To John Literman

With Best Wishes!

D. H. Byrd.

I'm an Endangered Species

D.H. Byrd

I'm an Endangered Species

The Autobiography of a Free Enterpriser

David Harold "Dry Hole" Byrd

Pacesetter Press
A Division of Gulf Publishing Company
Houston, Texas

**I'm an
Endangered
Species**

Library of Congress
Catalog Card Number
78-62614

ISBN 0-88415-258-8

Contents

Dedication

To independent wildcatters—
the oil finders who helped
make this country great

Acknowledgments

Beirne Lay, Jr., *Literary Consultant*
*James A. Clark, Mickey Herskowitz,
Bess Bond, *Research Assistance*

*deceased

I'm an Endangered Species

Chapter One

Introduction

By the time I was thirty years old, I had chalked up my first million dollars. On paper, that is. And I've been a millionaire ever since, sometimes on paper, but often with several million dollars cash in the bank.

The Almighty and this fabulous country of ours have been more than generous to me. There aren't too many places in the world where a boy who left college after two years to become a roughneck in the Texas oil fields (and among other things wrestle a carnival bear) could make it as big as I did at the rock bottom of the Great Depression in 1930 and through the frantic Roosevelt years leading up to World War II. There weren't many of the states other than Texas where this could have happened either.

The petroleum riches of the Lone Star State in the 1920s and 1930s put America on wheels, greased the gears of the whole stagnant economy, and became a decisive factor in winning against the Axis powers. Germany and Japan ran out of oil. We didn't.

It would be easy to say that Texas just lucked into its suddenly vital role in the nation's economy, firing our boilers when that was most needed. That the oil just happened to be there is only a partial reason. All the resources of the country have also been there waiting. But people tend to think of gasoline as something that shows up automatically at the pump at your local gas station. The fact is that the oil and natural gas that turn the country's wheels are a distillation of the guts—the blood, sweat and tears, and dry holes—of the independent oil men, teaming up with the major companies, who have waged a long battle to get gasoline to your pump and oil or natural gas into your home, without going broke.

That's what this book is about. At age seventy-seven, I've run the whole course. I'm getting kind of tired of being a whipping boy or an object of envy because I've made money at an honest trade. If it were legal, I wouldn't hesitate to "spoil" the scenery and put a drilling rig on the front lawn of my home in Dallas. It gets in your blood.

My central concern today is to shout from the rooftops, while I still can, against the government meddling that has beset the oil business for so long. The shortages of gas and oil to heat homes in the winter of 1976-77 were merely the predictable fruits of the well-intentioned, but bungling, chefs in Washington who have baked the indigestible cake of government controls on which the country is now choking.

I've managed to survive, despite the fact that a wildcatter strikes oil only one in ten tries. More money has been drilled into the ground in Texas than has been taken out of it, overall. There's a hoary saying that an oil man is a guy who "goes in the hole, and the deeper he goes in the hole, the deeper he goes in the hole."

After the great discovery of the East Texas oil field in 1930, I became the largest independent producer in the business, while maintaining a cooperative "dependence" on the major producers. In addition, I've run 52 companies, many of them in no way connected with oil.

It wasn't easy. I think I owe the reader, non-Texans, and anti-Texans with an envious chip on their shoulders a statement of my philosophy. It will emerge in due course. America should be eternally grateful to the independents. I should tell you how I got the nickname "Dry Hole" (for D.H.) Byrd. I drilled fifty-six dry holes before two new fields came in the same day, to change my luck for good. So that's the way it's been ever since.

Chapter Two

Roughneck

I'll tax your patience a little with a bit of family background, but I ought to say something about my pioneering urge. It was hereditary. And compulsive.

Certainly my cousin Admiral Richard E. Byrd of Virginia was a compulsive pioneer who became an explorer of the North and South Poles and a pioneer in aviation. In my prosperous years, I was able to help him in his ventures. He in turn is responsible for an American flag on the wall of my office in Dallas, that was flown over both Poles, later circling the earth many times aboard a Gemini spacecraft. There is also a map of Antarctica that shows the "Harold Byrd" Mountains, a range discovered by the Admiral 160 miles from the South Pole, and I also have a prized geological specimen from the region. Years later it gave me a strange feeling when I was poking around in the dry Taylor Valley in West Texas, many thousands of miles from the South Pole and stumbled onto a similar specimen of quartz-feldspar-mica granite.

Closer to home, my father Edward Byrd got the pioneer itch from predecessors who went west in 1799 into Missouri, still a part of the Louisiana Territory. Only nineteen years old, he migrated in a covered wagon in 1873 to the "promised land" of Texas, at Clarksville, in Lamar County. Liking what he saw, he returned to Missouri by pony to square himself away before moving permanently to Texas, winding up in the nearby village of Blossom.

In 1879, he married Mary (Mollie) Easley, a local farmer's daughter, built a small home, later added a cotton gin and a mill, several houses, and finally a store. Blossom became Byrd Town. Eventually, he moved to Detroit, Texas, where I was born on April 24, 1900, youngest of a family of five boys and three girls. He died in 1943, after living to see World War II half way to victory. He reached the ripe old age of eighty-eight, full of an insatiable curiosity about people and their place in the universe.

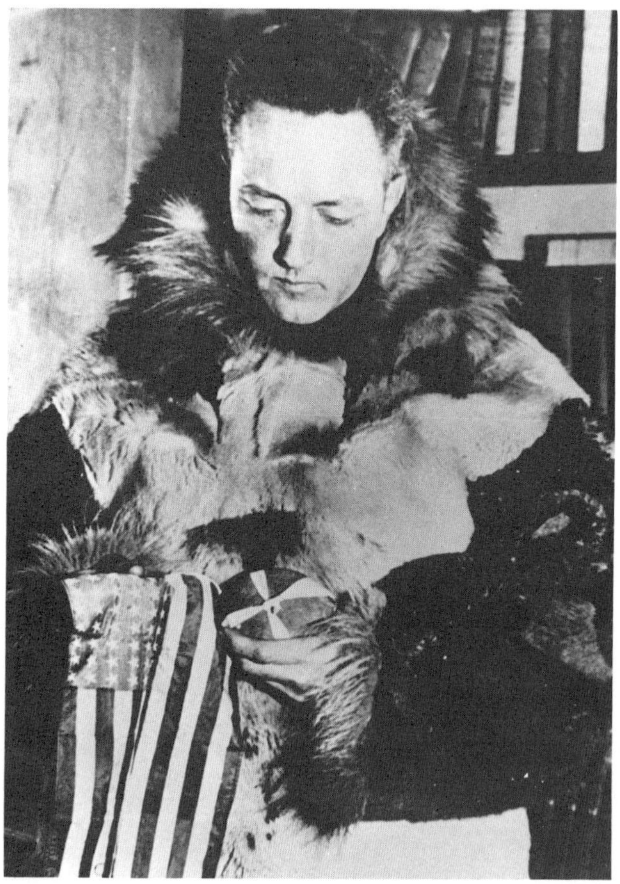

Admiral R.E. Byrd in expedition furs with "most traveled flag."

DHB

I idolized my father. By virtue of some built-in compass that always pointed to true North, he charted his course through the difficult years by relying on personal integrity above all else. I have tried hard to emulate his example in dealing with people from all walks of life.

My growing years in Byrd Town, Texas, and Ardmore, Oklahoma, our next new home, were happy ones. It was in many ways a more romantic age in America than today—simpler, but no easier than the stresses of modern living. A kind of lilac time before the Great War, World War I:

Seated Molly Easley Byrd and Edward Byrd, mother and father of (from left to right) Mary, R.J. (Leo), Harold, Burrette, and Lucille.

candy-striped shirts, paper collars, horse-drawn street cars. No social security other than your own savings account. The frontiers had been conquered, but the roads to undreamed of opportunity lay wide open and right under our feet, treasures of the earth waiting there to be uncovered by the hand and ingenuity of man.

But all that was still in the future. To most Americans, tomorrow meant another day of long, grinding work. Still, nobody told me I was "underprivileged" or working too hard, so I enjoyed myself to the hilt. My father set the pace. After a raging fire destroyed most of the town he had founded, he started over again in Ardmore, Oklahoma, just across the state line from Texas, where new opportunities beckoned. There he plunged into the treacherous waters of real estate, wheeling and dealing boldly. Among the properties he acquired was the local bottling works and a candy factory.

At age eleven, I got my first taste of business, literally, at the chocolate factory. They paid me 50¢ a Saturday to construct boxes for the candies. And the women who dipped the chocolate allowed me to lick their fingers. It was about as close to heaven as a small boy could get. My popularity with classmates in grammar school became immense: if you wanted your fill of candy at the factory, free, I was the man to see. Naturally, I presented boxes of candy to my girl friends, too. It backfired on me, though. I had a crush on Norma Scott and was keeping her well supplied until I discovered that I was subsidizing her boy friends. I stumbled on one of them enjoying an especially fine, large box of Norma's favorite assortment.

I thought about the bottle works for a bit and concluded that it needed more outlets. So, I persuaded kids from all over the neighborhood to set up soda pop stands, which I kept supplied, making my rounds with a wagon drawn by a pair of mules. It was a good arrangement. At my own pop stand under the sweltering sun, I was drinking up all my profits.

As a result of these early ventures in the system of free enterprise, I stumbled onto what might be termed The Byrd Principle—it is possible to combine fun with work in making money, and that turning a profit can be as exhilarating an experience as diving into the old water hole.

Encouraged by my parents, I got the habit early of keeping busy around the clock, in or out of school. On weekends and vacations I moved stock in the family grocery and drove the cows to pasture on the family spread outside Ardmore. It was a small herd, twenty-one cows, but I learned to open the gate while still in the saddle and trained the cattle to return to the corral without putting me to the trouble of dismounting.

In the clutch, my father always stood by me. I won't forget the time I was erroneously blamed for a shattered window at school. The evidence was circumstantial. A misguided bunch of the kids tried to lay the crime at my door. It looked as though I was in for a whipping or worse, when my father took me aside.

"Son," he asked earnestly, "did you do it?"

"No, sir," I answered, looking him square in the eye.

We went to the schoolmaster.

"Harold tells me he didn't do it," he told the man. "And he doesn't *lie.*"

That was the end of it.

DHB

After twelve years in Ardmore, my family moved once again, in 1913, to Midlothian, Texas. There, in 1929, the year that the stock market crashed, my parents were to celebrate their golden wedding anniversary. Their lives had mirrored the growing pains of an America that was no more. You could leaf through the pages of the Bible of such a family and see where our country had been and where it was going.

There was always music in the Byrd home, centering around my mother, a gentle soul with fierce inner strength. Her forte was the piano, my father's the banjo. One brother tried our patience practicing on the tuba, another scraped a violin, and both of my sisters, like their mother, were excellent pianists.

Since I settled for the drums, it became my duty to thump for the marching entrance going into school. Perhaps that may account for my zeal, much later, in seeing to it that the University of Texas could boast the biggest drum in the world for their football games.

I was a so-so student, with more curiosity about the world outside the classroom window than within the covers of an algebra book. Scouting, for instance. We had a damn good scoutmaster. On a hike, I'd try to see how many objects I could identify along the road, just looking ahead and really *seeing* a certain rock or outcropping. I can still identify and recall landmarks now when I'm driving and retrace my course over an area seen just once, without missing a turn.

When moving pictures came to town, I talked my way into a job as assistant operator at the only theater in Midlothian. The projector would break down or need rewinding with a new reel every fifteen or twenty minutes. That was my problem—that and the chore of sweeping out the gum wrappers and peanut shells between shows. You wouldn't believe, today, how eagerly and naively we waited for the next episode of Pearl White in *The Perils of Pauline,* struggling against her bonds on the railroad track with the locomotive bearing down on her ("continued next week"), or the paroxysms into which a young genius of silent comedy, Charles Chaplin, sent us, not to mention Harold Lloyd in *The Freshman.*

I recall William Jennings Bryan speaking passionately from the rear platform of a train, and, more to my liking, Buffalo Bill Cody and his wild west show, an annual fixture which I never missed. And Vernon Castle, World War I ace and showman, who danced with his wife Irene. Castle used to land his plane on a pea patch outside of town and take paying passengers up for their first hop. The sight of his Jenny, skimming beneath a white cumulus cloud, stirred something deep inside me. Some day, I swore to myself, airplanes would have to be a part of my experience.

DHB

Much as I looked up to my father, I guess he shared my esteem almost equally with my Uncle Ruddell (A. R. Byrd), a San Antonio businessman who owned an interest in more than a hundred banks plus a number of other profitable enterprises. One day Uncle Ruddell, who fancied himself a phrenologist, ran his hands over my head and prophesied:

"Harold, you're going to be the moneymaker of the family. You've got the ambition. But you've been no great shakes with your schoolbooks. I've got a proposition for you. If you become head of your class, I'll give you anything you name—within reason. Like a new bicycle."

That was all I needed to go to work on Miss Fish, our teacher, with a new-found craving for book lore, and what I hoped was charm and persuasion. Sure enough, in due course Uncle Ruddell received a document from Miss Fish attesting that David Harold Byrd was indeed at the head of his class. Uncle Ruddell was as good as his word, and I became the owner of a new bicycle, complete with mud guards. As for Miss Fish, may God have mercy on her white-lying soul.

"Tell me, Harold," Uncle Rudd then asked me, "What is the goal in your life that you most want to achieve?"

"I want to be president of my own company," I answered promptly. He nodded without comment apparently pleased, and I thought that the approving expression in his eyes was saying:

"You'll be the president of *more* than one company."

When the stock market crashed in 1929, Uncle Ruddell's old-fashioned sense of personal honor met the acid test and cost him a fortune. His four sons, to whom he had turned over his investments, now almost worthless, urged him to salvage what he could by going through bankruptcy. It was at a time when some men on Wall Street were solving similar crises by leaping from tall

From left to right, father, Edward Byrd, and Uncles Ruddell and William Byrd.

buildings, leaving their survivors to clean up the mess. Not Uncle Ruddell. He faced his sons.

"Our name has always stood for something," he said. "So there's only one thing to do. We'll sell the Alsop Process and pay back every cent that we owe."

The Alsop Process was a patented flour-whitening method which had been the family's untouchable anchor-to-windward since the old days back in Missouri. It was the sort of gold mine you never want to sell (it remains in use to this day).

The sons went along with their father's drastic solution, reminiscent of Sir Walter Scott's writing of the Waverley novels to pay back investors who had backed him in a banking venture, writing the endless pages by hand with numbed fingers in the icy cold of a castle in Scotland, until the last loser was reimbursed.

But Uncle Ruddell, now down to his three-story brick house in San Antonio and his private possessions, wasn't licked yet. A few years before his death, he mortgaged his home, bought an onion farm, and was so successful that he paid the bank back in a single year, and was able to leave his two daughters in comfortable circumstances.

With that sort of example before you at an impressionable age, when you grew up, you didn't need lawyers to hire other lawyers to keep *them* out of jail. A handshake was binding. Lawyers could take the time to work out the nitty-gritty later.

DHB

Football was one of my early passions. We played with a football as round as a cantaloupe, during and after school, on a field that had a kind of "artificial" surface—gravel. One flying tackle and you got skinned up pretty good. My specialty was drop-kicking. I used to drop-kick for lunch money, betting I could hit two out of three. Some days, but not often, I went hungry. In the evenings, we staged horse races, too, in a tough test of endurance over the two miles from the Byrd house to a standpipe two miles distant. I was the youngest and smallest jockey, and the luckiest.

For the most part, I was an obedient son. I tipped my hat to older men (not a universal custom) and polished my father's boots on Sunday mornings, then sat beside him in church. But I had a mind of my own, and there were limits to obedience. When my parents forbade me to have anything to do with the family of a gambler who had bought the house next door, I secretly rebelled and visited them anyway, because I couldn't see why the son and daughter, fine kids, should be penalized for their father's occupation.

When my father bought the first Model-T Ford in town, it put "Doc," our faithful, one-horsepower tractor out of a job pulling the family surrey. We decided to let Doc spend his declining years at a hotel we owned across the Red River in Madill, Oklahoma. I was nominated to ride him there. I was fourteen, and the two-day trip posed an adventure. Part way, I remember camping outside a home near the center of what would become downtown Dallas, under a sign that identified the family that had originally settled there: "Caruth 1848." What I didn't know was that inside that house, sleeping, was a little girl named Mattie (Martha) Caruth, who would one day become Mrs. David Harold Byrd.

After another day of hard riding I reached Madill, where my father was waiting and getting a bit anxious. He had learned that my mother had given me only $2.50 for expenses that included the toll for the ferry across the river.

I was indeed dead broke on my arrival at the hotel. But my father made it up by treating me to a royal feast.

DHB

There are a few more things that I should add about Edward Byrd, who was the kind of man most men would like to be but just don't find the time: scholar, rancher, merchant, explorer, naturalist. He had been trained as a mineralogist at Missouri University and acquired one of the country's first and finest rock collections, which he later donated to the University of Oklahoma.

The World Book Encyclopedia credits "Edward Byrd," a Kansas prospector," with drilling the first producing well in Oklahoma, near Chelsea, in 1899. Although the family records are sketchy on this point, it is likely that Edward Byrd struck his gusher while still traveling out of Missouri (not Kansas), still undecided on his future, the year I was born in 1900. The point is that with his background it was scarcely surprising that he aroused my interest in geology at an early age, explaining to me how certain rocks were formed and what they represented in minerals.

Looking back, I would say that my boyhood ended when my father's fortunes suffered a heavy blow just at a time when it seemed that our financial security was assured, and he had retired.

Father had endorsed the note of the Ardmore Wholesale Grocery Company, which went broke. Being the only man who had anything, he paid off about $40,000 (a fortune in those days) and took over. I helped him in the gloomy chore of sorting what was left of the stock for sale.

I was in for a rough time. But it would be the making of me.

DHB

When it really sank in on me that father had lost his money, I went out into the oil fields at Burkburnett in the summer and roughnecked from midnight until noon the next day.

On my day off, I worked for my brother, who ran a jitney line from Midlothian to Waxahachie. Then, after my brother went off to the World War I, he turned the jitney line over to another fellow who let me drive the service car during my time off from the oil fields.

Lots of times I'd drive until midnight, skip bed altogether and go straight to the rigs. Not that a bed was any great luxury. Landlords rented beds in eight-hour shifts, and they were still damp with your predecessor's sweat when you turned in, benumbed with fatigue. Once, a stranger paid me $50 to drive him through the rain and mud from Burkburnett to Newton, a distance of eight miles. It took me four hours and two tire changes.

DHB

For a boy of seventeen, I found myself struggling to hold my own in pretty rough, sometimes violent, company, known as "wildcatters," a term dating back to the nineteenth century, when the first Pennsylvania oil explorers were said to be "heading for wildcat country."

There must have been about 40,000 of them, mostly poor and uneducated farmers' and ranchers' sons who had been drawn to Texas in the hope of making big money. Not many got rich, but if what they were looking for was also in the form of gambling, liquor, easy ladies, and brawls in abundance, they had come to the right place.

For me, it was a major adjustment, in an environment in which I wanted to, and did, survive, but of which I did not care to become a typical specimen. I had more serious goals than hell-raising. One of these was to improve my education, go to college if possible. I received a strong pitch from Homer Garrison, from Waxahachie, an old friend whom I had confronted in high school debates, to join him at the University of Texas. But I could not yet afford it and advanced my education in other ways.

I took secretarial courses at Metropolitan College in Dallas (shorthand, bookkeeping, and typing), earning my tuition in part by nursing a mental patient whose mother was afraid to be left alone with him at night. I found out why when I was awakened at five o'clock one morning with a knife at my throat. My gut instincts told me that he must be under some hallucination that I was a threat to him, instead of an ally trying to help him. Talking along that line, I was able to calm him down, coax him back into bed, and hide the knife. Gradually gaining his trust, I got to where I could handle him without trouble, and I was no longer afraid. I never told my family about it.

DHB

The University of Texas was still my first choice, but there was a small college nearer home, Trinity College, in which I enrolled as a first step. I went out for baseball and discovered that I had a knack for pitching. In fact, I had a fast ball that smoked. In my sophomore year I was the starting pitcher in a spring-training exhibition game against a top team in the National League, the Chicago Cubs. Their manager was Frank Evers of the immortal double-play combination of Tinkers-to-Evers-to-Chance. And they had a fearsome long-ball hitter named Burleigh Grimes.

Here was an opportunity, heaven-sent, to show off my fireball where it might count later on. I pitched my arm out, not even bothering in my excitement to wear a warm-up jacket between innings. That was an oversight that would cost me the dream of earning a varsity letter when I transferred to the University of Texas. My pitching muscles stiffened up on me.

Still optimistic that the arm was recovering, I threw a few pitches for the Texas coach, "Uncle" Billy Disch; understandably, I was nervous. Disch was considered one of the keenest baseball minds in the game.

After a few pitches, Disch walked over, took the ball and rubbed it in his hands, then gave me a puzzled look.

"Done much pitching, Byrd?" he asked.

"Well, sir," I answered rather proudly, "I pitched for the Texas All-Stars against the Chicago Cubs in an exhibition game."

"I'm afraid you threw your arm away," he said sadly. "You don't have anything left, son." He was right.

I was heartbroken, but the hurt was to be assuaged years later when the University awarded me an honorary letterman's blanket with the varsity "T" on it—the first such exception, I'm told, in forty years.

I doubt that any honor will ever please me more, although I was also to be voted an honorary alumnus and a distinguished alumnus of the University, and a life member of the Dad's Club.

Frustrated in baseball, I tried wrestling, eventually winning the 145-pound championship of the University, a cauliflower ear, and something of a reputation. I also won a spot on the Glee Club singing tenor. We knew nearly everybody by sight or by name, and I acquired a lifelong affection for my alma mater in that intimate era when the focal point of all campus activity was the "Old B Hall," a rambling wooden structure of three stories.

Naturally, I majored in geology, coupling theory with practical experience during summer vacation as a roughneck, learning to be a floor man, fireman, tool dresser, and gauge man on a rig at Santa Anna, Texas.

I was already under something of a cloud with my fellow workers as a "college man." The beneficiary of higher education was deemed a smartass and usually mistrusted on sight. A friend from Texas Christian University didn't help matters when he leaked the information that I was a college wrestling champion. When the skeptical crew at the rig were loath to take this information at face value, I quickly found myself in the position of putting my money where my friend's mouth was.

A wiry fellow named Slim eagerly rose to the challenge of trimming me down to size. As for myself, I wagered my entire earnings on the outcome.

It took me ninety-six seconds to pin Slim.

The victory was sweet, but it generated a new problem. Later, when a carnival came to town advertising a wrestling bear with a reward of $100 for anyone who could throw the bear, I was the automatic choice.

How could I refuse? I weighed my chances carefully. The bear would be muzzled, chained, and wearing boxing gloves over his forepaws. But the chain was long enough to give him considerable mobility, and he wouldn't need his teeth or his claws to win. My best hold in wrestling had always been the leg scissors. But how do you apply the scissors to a bear that weighs 300 pounds? It seemed a losing game, at best, but my competitive instinct won out and I determined to give it my best shot.

The bear eyed me warily with his small, squinty eyes as I moved in on the critter, grabbing him and maneuvering for a chance to apply the scissors. But the bear got one paw loose and fetched me a clout alongside the temple that sent me reeling across and out of the ring. Helpful friends cleared my senses with a bucket of water, but my ears didn't stop ringing for a long time.

DHB

After a wonderful two years at the University of Texas, I painfully faced up to the necessity of dropping out and going to work full time. The "shortest, gladdest years of life," for me, were over.

I was especially distressed at not being able to complete the full course in geology. But at least I had a solid foundation that was to serve me well.

That word "geology," by the way, covers a heck of a lot of ground and has helped me to this day in getting a broad look at all the forms of energy from which we may have to choose soon to supplement petroleum products. Coal—the country has enough to last about five hundred years. Nuclear power—tremendously expensive, thanks in part to the conservationists, but with a correspondingly tremendous potential. For Japan and France, for instance, it is already a must; they have no oil. Solar energy—promising but still in the future. The problem is how to convert sunlight directly into electricity in large enough quantities to meet the need. Windmills—promising with 200-foot rotors, but subject to wide variations in output, and still costly. The tides—promising, but also high in initial cost. The tides have already been harnessed on the coast of France at the English Channel to produce electricity, and a study for the harnessing of the huge tides in the Bay of Fundy was laid aside only when inexpensive gas and oil seemed preferable. Geothermal—already in common use for heating at no cost for fuel, but for power plants the steam is not normally hot enough, and the impurities in the underground hot water foul up the electric generating machinery.

As a "nongraduate" but lifelong enthusiastic geologist, I find myself rooting for all these alternatives. We can't do the whole job with petroleum products, although the government can measurably prolong our resources with wiser policies to encourage exploration for new oil.

Chapter Three

The Big Time

The nearest approach to government "interference" in the oil business during the 1920s, when my career as an independent operator began, was the creation of the Texas Railroad Commission in 1919. But the interference was minimal, concerned mainly with prohibiting waste through measures such as "spacing" limits on how close a well could be to another well. But even then, the granting of "exceptions" was the rule rather than the exception.

Thus, it was open season for the wildcatter and the wheeler dealer operating in the free market environment of supply and demand. Price controls were unheard of. True, in 1924, President Coolidge was concerned enough about the government's responsibility for the protection of a growing natural resource against waste to establish an Oil Conservation Board. Basing its report on the findings of the American Petroleum Institute, it came up with the verdict that there was "no waste." Everybody in the business knew that this was a lie.

"There *was* great waste and, under existing drilling practices, a grave danger of exhausting reserves."*

In 1927, Humble Oil introduced voluntary "proration" in a large field, limiting production. The Texas Railroad Commission followed suit by extending voluntary prora-

---

*James A. Clark and Michel T. Halbouty, *The Last Boom.* Random House: New York, 1972.

tion (regulation of output) to a second field. It made sense then and still does.

Likewise, I have no quarrel with federal intervention (through martial law in 1931) to call a halt to the abuses associated with "hot oil," shipped at cut-rate prices out of state in violation of "allowable production." To the relief of all concerned, the Connally Act of 1935 prohibited the sale of hot oil in interstate commerce. But the ambitions of Secretary of the Interior Harold L. Ickes to institute federal price controls through the NIRA (National Industrial Recovery Administration) were checked by a ruling of the U.S. Supreme Court that such controls were invalid.

It was nearly twenty years later, in 1954, before federal meddling began to harass the petroleum industry following a landmark decision by the Supreme Court that the Federal Power Commission had authority to fix prices of natural gas in interstate commerce at the wellhead. I wrote in vain to numerous congressmen and to President Eisenhower, who vetoed a decontrol bill.

I mention all this briefly as background for my own fortunes as an independent and to underscore my lifelong opposition to price controls. They've never worked, and they never will. As for the free market, it has never failed us, and no better system has ever been devised.

DHB

My first goal was to head my own company, but this would have to wait. I didn't have the capital. Still, there were other ways to go for a young man anxious to get started. Where possible, the idea was to operate with other people's money.

My first model was a man considered by many to be the greatest wheeler dealer ever to hit the oil patch, named Colonel A.E. Humphreys, who was riding the crest of a wild boom in Mexia, Texas. My brother had found work there and urged me to "come on down, the money's good."

At first, Humphreys paid me $7.50 per day as a tool dresser and boilerman. Then I moved up to a gauger's position (measuring potential oil flow in a well) and helped bring in the Tom Berthenson well.

For a roughneck only twenty-three years old, I figured I was doing okay. Colonel Humphreys must have observed something he liked in my approach to the job, for he assigned me to work with his chief geologist, Julius Fohs, as a geological scout, working out of Houston. I got my salary up to $300 per month.

Often dispensing with a night's sleep, I scouted the drilling wells over a wide area, virtually living in a company car. Once, after being late in returning the car to the motor pool, I was bawled out by the office manager. Humphreys happened to overhear the reprimand and intervened.

"Dammit, Byrd's the best scout we have," he said. "Give him *my* car."

So, out of a fleet of 200 company cars I was given license number one.

I made a special study of the Balcones fault zone, saving samples taken at ten-foot intervals to help me to decide where to set the casing. I believe I was the first geologist to do this. I'd go up to a location with a figure in my head of, say, 2250 feet. I'd add the elevation, pick the spot, and we'd commence drilling. At the other end of the field we'd have a different figure, and we were drilling or spudding in a new well about every other day.

DHB

In my capacity as a geologist and troubleshooter for Humphreys I began to build something of a reputation. I decided it was time to get my feet wet on my own. Obtaining a twenty-acre lease that offset the Deusenberg well, I brought in a winner that produced 23,000 barrels and was bought by the Magnolia Company on the strength of information I was able to give them. Out of the profits, they erected the Magnolia Building in Dallas.

I sold my lease for $86,000 to a group that was committed to drilling only to a specified depth. They came up empty, but when a new group took over, and I had lost my interest, they drilled fifty-six feet deeper and brought in a 5,000 barrel well. I made a vow to myself never to give up on a well without pushing fifty-six feet deeper.

Three times, after going temporarily broke, I returned to Colonel Humphreys. He always gave me a job, no questions asked. His continued confidence was as welcome as the paycheck.

I financed the first of my fifty-six dry holes as a wildcatter by selling leases at $1000 an acre in the Currie area forty-five miles north of Mexia, on Woodbine oil sand, with excellent prospects. We hit salt water. Subsequently, a luckier party brought in a field right alongside it.

I never sold stock, but raised capital by buying and selling leases and by joining forces with larger companies. As an example, I leased 10,000 acres in Zavala County from Colonel Ike Pryor of San Antonio, reselling 1000 acres of it to the Humble Company. Then I parlayed Humble's purchase order as a credit to buy a rig, and sold a half-interest in the well to E.L. Doheny for $86,000.

Once, Doheny and I, as partners, brought in a major gas well. In those days before pipelines encouraged mass consumption, natural gas was pretty much worthless; I was ahead of the hounds. Only three years later, Claude Witherspoon took over the leases, bored more holes, built a pipeline to San Antonio, and opened up a new fuel source for the city.

DHB

Why did investors continue to string along with a loser like Byrd? Part of the answer is that I was ahead of the state of the art in drilling machinery. A depth of 3,000 feet was about the limit when we drilled by rotary and brought the well in by cable tools. The first good hole drilled in Mexia, for example, required nearly two years to get down to 3,000 feet.

A great many of my "dry" holes were subsequently reopened with deeper-drilling techniques (today they go to nearly 30,000 feet). So there was nothing seriously wrong about my geology that couldn't have been cured by a better rig. Anyway, the odds were about ten to one against you, so my backers didn't expect miracles.

There was another factor that kept me going, besides my inherent stubbornness. I insisted upon incorporating into my deals a retainer fee in cash. It was substantial enough so that I couldn't really lose, whether the well was a gusher or dry.

Only once did I come close to complete discouragement during those years of uncertainty. I was down close to my last few dollars and needed new clothes. That was one item it was poor business to skimp on. A friendly tailor in Dallas was willing to sell me three suits on credit, and on the same day I had lunch with a business prospect and not enough money to pick up the tab. It is the only time in my life that I had to out fumble the other guy. He paid.

It hurt my pride. Painfully.

After leaving Humphreys for the last time, I set up shop as a consulting geologist at $100 per day—no paltry sum during the Depression. It wasn't steady work, but I was now in a strategic position to make some real money.

Without the major oil companies' confidence in my ability to find oil, I doubt that I would have scored the successes that I did. These same companies, and others, are the ones that Congress seems intent on destroying by shortsighted over-regulation that destroys risk taking at the source. I doubt seriously that 5% of our lawmakers could come up with an understandable definition of "statutory depletion."

DHB

The good ship "Byrd" finally came in. On the same day, May 5, 1928, first the Byrd and Daniels well blew in, making a thousand barrels a day ($3.00 per barrel) at the Santa Anna field in Coleman County. I had offered acreage around her to fifteen different oil companies, with no takers. Company geologists were a much more conservative lot than us wildcatters, and I couldn't resist rubbing it in a bit when a company big wig asked me condescendingly, before the news had spread, how I was coming along with my well.

"It's not producing sand," was all I told him.

Then, before the day was out, another gusher blew in, opening up the Baker Gas Field in Brown County.

I was on my way.

Next, on August 20, 1930, the Byrd and Harman Discovery Well in the Scurry County Pool, at Ira, Texas, came in. It was producing thirty-one barrels a day when the rig burned out. I cleaned the well, installed new casing and continued to get thirty-one barrels a day. It never varied, just that thirty-one barrels. The big play was only five miles away. Mine happened to be a crevice well.

I kept on plugging away, devoting a lot of my time and energy to the East Texas area being neglected by the skeptical experts of the major companies. During my travels there I began acquiring a large number of leases.

It was a good thing I did.

DHB

Fate was to bring my path across that of an eccentric character named Columbus Marion Joiner (later known as "Dad"), a friend of my father's. Geologists James A. Clark and Michel T. Halbouty, in their classic book *The Last Boom,* have well described Dad Joiner and the climate of the times, as follows:

> A bit of a charlatan, a bit of a poet, something of a dreamer and always a promoter, Columbus Marion Joiner shambled back and forth across Rusk County, Texas (about a hundred miles east of Dallas) during the 1920s telling anyone who would listen that the drought-stricken fields and pine-studded hills were floating on an ocean of oil. He was an old wildcatter, bent by his years,

by a crippling illness, and by a harsh decade of unrelieved failure, but his hymn of hope was the only song in an area where depression had been an economic constant since the end of World War I.

Only the poor listened. They listened, and they believed because they needed desperately to believe. When he spoke to them in their farmyards, they gazed out across their stunted corn and ravelling cotton and envisioned derricks sprouting from the parched and cracking earth.

They believed against all reason. In the past, other wildcatters and established oil companies had drilled seventeen dry holes in the county. Scientists for major oil companies had examined every foot of the land with every modern oil-seeking device and almost to a man had condemned it. The few geologists who were not completely convinced that Rusk County was barren of oil were not heeded in the oil company board rooms.

But while the oil companies frowned on Rusk and neighboring counties, speculators in distant cities had caught the postwar oil fever. Discovery of rich fields on the Gulf Coast and in North Central Texas apparently had convinced them that a hole punched anywhere in the Lone Star State would spout oil. Time and time again promoters acquired oil leases on thousands of Rusk County acres to sell to speculators. Almost without exception the purchasers allowed the leases to expire or they grew tired of paying rentals when no successful wells were drilled.

DHB

I was one of the believers in Dad Joiner. It was partly faith in my own geological observations of the East Texas area and partly because of the sheer doggedness of the man's adherence to what seemed to be more than just a hunch. He was fully convinced of the truth of his own prophecies that he would usher in the greatest oil field in the history of America.

When I learned that Dad had invested well over a year, using beat-up machinery that was constantly breaking down and being repaired by his extraordinarily resourceful driller, Ed Laster, in charge of a pick-up crew, I knew that the time had come to act. Without some first-rate equipment, Joiner and Laster stood little or no chance of bringing in a well at the very moment that it was showing promise. Ed Laster's bit had chewed into samples of oil-bearing Woodbine sand, but the hole would have to be reamed out and widened before drilling could proceed deeper for the payoff.

I arranged to lend the needed machinery and had it shipped in from Elkhart, Texas, for installation under the rickety old derrick. The well was known as the "Daisy Bradford 3" (it had been relocated a small distance twice) after the widow on whose farm Joiner had spudded it in.

Daisy Bradford's farm was near Longview, Texas. I packed up and headed for Longview.

Chapter Four

The Summit Achieved

The big day had arrived at the Daisy Bradford 3 well—October 5, 1930.

I was there with my gauges, just in case, along with several thousand spectators who had arrived at the scene two days previously, to watch Ed Laster drill out the cement plug at the bottom of the casing so that bailing could commence. Delays had continued to harass him.

> It was like a religious revival or a great camp meeting. The throng was optimistic, enthusiastic, and good-natured. Bootleggers mixed with the devout and sold pints of white lightning and pop-skull, which helped keep the chilling wind from biting too deeply into some.
>
> "But where's Dad Joiner?" someone asked, and the question went the rounds. Joiner was not to be found. Ed Laster could not be asked; he and the crew were busy sending the bailer into the well and bringing it up laden with mud and water. By relieving the pressure of the mud and water on the oil sand, Laster hoped to coax oil to the surface. But the oil did not come.
>
> Word spread that Joiner was ill in Dallas, and a moan of sympathy sounding like wind through the trees burst forth from the crowd. But Joiner was not really ill. He was aware of the ever-growing suspicions about his wheelings and dealings, and he didn't want to face those who might look on him with loathing and contempt. At the very time the well might be coming in, he didn't want to answer questions as to how it had been accomplished.

All through that day Laster and his crew ran the bailer without a show of oil. When darkness fell, lanterns were lighted and the work continued until the crew was exhausted and Laster signalled for a halt.

When the work resumed the next morning, the people were there . . . By ten o'clock Laster had bailed the hole as free of mud and water as possible, and still there was no show of oil. At that moment, as if on signal, a murmur went through the crowd. "Dad Joiner's coming through," someone said, and they made way for their hero. They patted him on the back and shouted welcomes to him as he wormed his way through the vast assembly of people and vehicles. He returned the cheers with a smile and a wave.

He climbed through the wire fence Laster had now erected to keep the people from getting too near the derrick. He mounted the rig floor, and the crowd cheered him as he conferred with Laster. They continued cheering him as he left the floor and joined "Dry Hole" Byrd, his young wildcatter friend who had supplied the new machinery for the rig.

Laster and the crew began "swabbing" the well. The swab was a steel and rubber device which was attached to a steel cable and lowered into the hole. It fitted snugly inside the casing, and was open at the bottom so that it could go through mud and water. After it had been lowered to the depth Laster determined proper, he would begin to draw it from the hole. Its bottom opening would close and the vacuum created was supposed to pull the oil from the Woodbine. But with each swab the word that came from the rig was "nothing yet."

Night came and the lanterns were lighted again. "Nothing yet," Laster said as the swab again brought mud and water flying from the hole. Again he shut down the rig for the night.

The next day, October 5, was a Sunday, and daylight found many of the devout on their way to churches to pray for the well's success. Still, there were never less than 5,000 present during the day as Laster and the crew continued swabbing. Joiner was glassy-eyed with fatigue and strain. Laster and the crewmen were short-tempered. The professional oilmen had long ago decided that if the well did come in it would not be a big one. But the farmers and town folk never wavered in their faith. When firewood for the boilers was exhausted, farmers ripped tires from their old trucks and offered them as fuel. The stench of burning rubber rose to high heaven, but the work went on.

It was late in the evening when Laster, drawing the swab from the casing, heard a gurgling sound deep in the hole. He spun around, shouting, "Put out the fires! Put out your cigarettes! *Quick!*"

Those nearest the rig felt a slight trembling of the earth. The gurgle became a roar. Suddenly a column of oil and water shot high above the derrick. It spread out like a titan's umbrella and fell down upon the pressing crowd like a torrent of raindrops . . .

When he decided it was free of mud and water, Laster spun the valves and directed the oil into one of the tanks. There was quiet. Joiner asked Dry Hole Byrd to gauge the flow. "Whisper it to me," he said. Byrd got his gauges and went to the tank. When he returned he whispered in Joiner's ear, "She's flowing at the rate of sixty-eight hundred barrels a day!"

Joiner gasped. Without thinking he shouted high above the noises of the crowd, "Sixty-eight hundred barrels! Unbelievable!" . . . Joiner's shout had let the cat out of the bag. This was no dinky well, it was a whopper . . . Dad Joiner had kept the faith.*

DHB

For me, the next few weeks became a blur. The name of the game had become "leases."

---

*James A. Clark and Michel T. Halbouty, *The Last Boom.* Random House: New York, 1972.

Actually, I was already in pretty deep. I had been on the scene for a couple of years, buying cheap leases for $1.00 per acre plus a 50-cent brokerage fee. Now they were worth several thousand dollars an acre, and I controlled the Lathrop and Kilgore blocks and one other.

Out of a 15,000 acre block in Kilgore, about 5,000 acres were good for oil and on the eastern side the land was good for gas. I planned to sell a half-interest. When Humble hesitated, I sold a quarter to Gulf. Soon Wallace Pratt of Humble was on the phone.

"We hear you made a deal with Gulf today," he said, "after you left us. We want to get in and I'll take that quarter now."

"It'll cost you twice as much as Gulf paid," I said, "because I don't need to sell now."

I went down and closed the deal.

DHB

One of my first concerns was titles. I had to work fast. After renting office space in the Gregg Hotel in Longview, strategically located, I secretly bought out the Gregg Abstract Company operated by Hall Wood and tied up all five notaries public who were active in the county.

I also got approval from the county to erect several temporary office structures on the courthouse lawn.

Some questions may naturally jump into the reader's mind. Did I use political pull? Did I buy people off? Did I get away with anything unethical?

All the answers are "no." I had every right to buy out the abstract company while keeping it discreetly quiet. No political influence was needed to make use of the courthouse lawn; the county was only too happy to grant me its permission, since I would be helping them to cope with a huge surge of business that threatened to swamp them.

It was a case, pure and simple, of "getting thar fustest with the mostest," by thinking faster and farther ahead than the competition, when the stakes were enormous.

I gained a further edge on the field by racing to Dallas in my Pierce Arrow and hiring seventy-two girl typists, assigning one girl to each volume of titles.

As soon as the courthouse opened each morning, on my instructions the girls would rush into the county clerk's office and each would claim the volume to which I had assigned her. Thus, I had the books, the notaries and the title companies. Practically every lease transaction had to pass through hands controlled by me. I'd meet the notaries at a certain point with my lease men and then we'd go out and make a block.

"But wait a minute," you may say, "what about those notaries? Weren't they supposed to be serving the public impartially as "notaries public"? Again, the answer is that I paid the going rate—no more—and the notaries, dependent on their fees, merely chose to go where the action was. I happened to be at the hub of the activity. And I paid cash. Right now. The notaries, of course, were available to anyone else, but the upshot was that I got priority.

I learned the value of showmanship. That Pierce Arrow, for example, was a real selling tool and became a symbol. It exuded an aura of MONEY. In eight months I put 86,000 miles on the odometer—seven years' normal driving.

I wasn't winning any popularity contests with these tactics, except among my clients, but to the disgruntled my answer was "I'm not stopping anyone from getting their titles cleared. I'm just getting mine cleared first."

I made it a point to carry $10,000 in cash in my wallet every day so that I could pay off people in hard money. It

The Pierce Arrow that was my "calling card." It was said that if the owner of the Pierce Arrow told you he would buy your lease, he *would* buy it. So, it was better than having money in the bank.

really made their eyes bulge. And it enabled me to take a lot of leases away from Standard Oil, which paid by check.

I was able to guarantee same-day service to nearly everyone on leases. My office in the Gregg Hotel lobby had a window opening on an alley. We did a brisk business through that window, taking in documents, paying out cash and checks. When I found acreage I wanted, I could have it investigated by evening and pay off the lease seller immediately.

At one time I owned 34,000 acres, but sold parts of it and ended up owning 15,000 acres in partnership with Gulf, Humble, and Atlantic Oil Companies, with whom I drilled about 5,000 wells. During the great boom, my wheeler dealing in leases, in itself, was almost as profitable as owning an oil well. Needless to say, I became an overnight millionaire.

I was still to come up with the inevitable dry well, though no longer in discouraging streaks. I drilled also in Kansas, Oklahoma, and Missouri during the 1930s, sinking one dry hole that later opened up a big field. There were enough oil-bearing holes, though, to keep my appetite whetted.

However, in 1931, I also had my problems. Like a couple of hundred potential lawsuits from transactions that have to be consummated in a big hurry. My policy, if anyone had a legitimate beef, was to pay the aggrieved party a fair settlement and stay out of court. Not everyone, however, played the game the same way, notably one B. A. "Barney" Skipper, who gave me a real shafting.

I accused him of reneging on an agreement to deliver certain leases to me.

"You've signed this map," I told him, "and you agreed to deal. If it had been a dry hole I'd have had to pay off, so I'm expecting delivery."

"No way," Skipper answered, bridling.

"You mean you're going to be a crooked son of a bitch?" I asked in disbelief. Skipper, at least was forthright.

"Sure, I'll be that and anything else you want to call me, he said, "because there's a million dollars in it for me!"

I started for him, determined to knock the hell out of him, but others who were present broke it up.

Maybe it was just as well. My lawyer subsequently advised me that I would probably have lost in court on the grounds that leases can be transferred only in writing.

I never got delivery of the leases, which is how Barney Skipper got his start.

DHB

Others who made it big in the mad confusion of the discovery of the huge East Texas field were H. L. Hunt, who sewed up all of Dad Joiner's rights in return for assuming responsibility for lawsuits on Joiner's manipulations (Dad had been like the prizefighter who sells 150% of himself to backers), J. M. Crim, Walter Lechner, Ray Hubbard, and John Farrell and his associates.

The new oil field, when fully explored, proved out to be a reservoir about forty-five miles long by five to twelve miles wide (140,000 acres), the greatest ever seen on the American continent.

I'm sure that other people would welcome the same problem, but how does a man cope with overnight success? It would have been easy to have made an ass of myself, satisfying every errant whim. I made up my mind to try to do otherwise with the rest of my life. Rightly or wrongly, I told myself, "You're better than that."

Chapter Five

Master Plan

Not many people are fortunate enough to be able at some point to just sit down and map out their whole future. For me, the year 1931 was such an opportunity.

As head of my own organization, Byrd-Frost, Inc. (Jack Frost was my close partner for several years, including during my East Texas operations), I had a solid base. My enterprises, when at their height, would require three floors of office space in the Tower Petroleum Building.

High on my list was the University of Texas. Despite my enforced drop-out after two years, I have nursed an abiding affection for the "Forty Acres" and its fortunes, especially on the football field. Wealth would enable me to play the generous "old grad" to the hilt.

Secondly, I wanted to follow up on my infatuation with the airplane, inspired by those early flights of barnstormer Vernon Castle. I did so, earning my pilot's license under the instruction of Art Gobel, who sold me an Eaglerock—the first of a long string of aircraft for business and private use. I was to become active in airport development and an early sponsor of the Civil Air Patrol, and as previously mentioned, of Admiral Byrd's flights to the two Poles.

Another goal was to reach a rapport with the politicians who ran things, especially at the seat of state government in Austin, although I had no aspirations for public office. Sam Rayburn, Morrie Sheppard, John Connally, and Lyndon Johnson on the national scene were to become men

I could go to at any time that I wanted action, and so were a succession of Texas governors. Among the ablest was John Connally, a man of singular integrity and strong convictions that cross party lines, who says he's in my debt for pleading his cause at every opportunity with beautiful Ida Nell (Nellie) Brill, Sweetheart of The University of Texas in 1940. At any rate, she chose him from a formidable list of rivals. Connally was president of the student body. When I saw him recently in Houston he said he wasn't "running for anything." I only wish he were President of the United States.

I have always been gregarious, loved big parties—the bigger the better—and good Scotch. I wanted to be a welcome member of Dallas society. And eventually get married.

My old friend, the late President Lyndon B. Johnson, and I at a University of Texas football game in the Cotton Bowl, Dallas, Texas.

I won't say, in the words ascribed to a Lubbock society matron, that I was "just nuts about culture," but I had a genuine interest in music and musicians and a flair for sculpture and painting, to which I turned my hand much later in life. I was an early booster and close friend of pianists Van Cliburn and Jose Iturbi.

Certainly not least among the outlets which money would enable me to indulge were fishing and hunting, including safaris in Africa and tiger hunts in Sumatra. I loved travel, in itself.

In all honesty, I must confess that whether by design or accident, I was to evolve into what people from other parts of the country visualize as the archetype of the Texas oil millionaire or "oillionaire." They would doubtless accuse me of being boastful, loud, and enamored of "bigness" for its own sake, and I might as well plead "guilty as charged."

Van Cliburn (at age 7) with mother and father and Martha Byrd.

My "hunting buddy," General Jim Doolittle and I on safari, South Africa.

My esteemed friend and hunting and fishing partner, General Jim Doolittle (he prefers "Jim" to "Jimmy"), once paid me the left-handed compliment of describing me to a mutual acquaintance in these words "I'll give Byrd this much. He's every bit as good as he *says* he is."

This appraisal may stem from our hunting trips. I consider him a crack shot, and he returns the compliment. And it is possible that he has an exaggerated admiration for my skill with tricks of magic. On one of our tiger hunting trips in Sumatra I astonished the natives with card tricks and prestidigitations with coins and other objects. What I didn't tell Jim was that during my younger days in Dallas I had joined a magician's club which in turn had affiliations with professional magicians who met in Chicago. We exchanged trade secrets and vied with each other, using both prepared tricks and dexterity. With the advantage of being an "insider," it was easy for me to confound the General along with the gullible Sumatrans.

A word more about Doolittle, who is best known to the public as a pilot, aeronautical engineer, military commander, and adviser to presidents on scientific and defense matters. The salient characteristic of his that sticks most in my mind is that he is the only man I ever knew who is absolutely fearless. He doesn't know what fear is, literally. He even admits it, (If pressed, I too will admit no animal fear of wild beasts and damn little of anything else.) That trait, plus skill, explains why he survived so many emergencies in the air.

Having a fondness for being Number One in all my undertakings, it doesn't come naturally for me to confess that Doolittle is the one man whom I would gladly serve in any venture as Number Two. I am grateful to have a "national institution" for a friend.

Once, on safari in Africa, I was approaching my baited blind at night when there came the unmistakable growl of a tiger, dangerously close. My English guide, Thompson, called to me in alarm to run for it!

"I can't run," I called back, "but I can *shuffle.*"

Making as good time as possible (my joints were no longer young), I managed to reach safety. When I recounted this to Doolittle, he considered it coolness under fire.

After "arriving" as a full-fledged Texas millionaire, I may have seemed to be enjoying the role of a sort of Jolly Green Giant. But when I search my soul, I find that my greatest satisfaction has been, where possible, in trying to help my fellow man, a satisfaction which Doolittle also says he rates the highest.

When you deal with people, if for no better reason than because it's good business, you want a fellow to come back for more.

(text continued on page 44)

Hunting wild game is a slow and, often, frustrating process, so taking a beautiful trophy, like this leopard I shot in Kenya, is truly rewarding.

In big game hunting it pays one to be a crack shot and able to take down an animal, like this lion I bagged in South Africa, cleanly and quickly.

DHB

The best thing I could do for the University of Texas, I decided, was by way of loans. The first ground rule was that the candidate could not otherwise have afforded a college education.

My second rule was not to delegate the selections but to personally interview each prospect. If I felt that he, or in some cases, she, was good material, I'd say, "I'm willing to bet on you. If you let me down, I'll throw in my hand."

Results were mixed. In most cases the student chalked up a commendable record and received my standard graduation gift: I tore up the note for the amount of the loan. But in the cases of those who failed to cut the mustard, I left the loans in force.

Two of my beneficiaries turned out to be Olympic track champions. Boyce Gatewood, the high hurdler, and Eddie Southern, the quarter-miler, were blessed with a speed on the track which was not reflected in the repayment of their obligations to me. But at least Gatewood (whose sister I also helped through school) eventually redeemed himself. On graduation, he had gone into the Navy without touching base with me, finished his four-year stint, returned to Dallas.

When he strode into my inner office, he asked, "Would you mind kicking me in the ass?"

"It will be a pleasure," I answered.

He assumed the stance and I delivered a hard boot to the seat of his trousers. Straightening up, he reached in his pocket and handed me a check for $700, the principal of the loan plus interest.

The other track man never did crash through. But nearly all those people eventually at least thanked me. It still galls me that I have never heard from Eddie Southern. By contrast, there is Bernie J. Esunas, who lettered in football and pulled a tour in the Air Force after graduation. I attended his wedding and still get a card from him on every Father's Day. He's become a prosperous oil man.

I well remember one girl who needed help. She showed me the house where her mother supported them both by taking in washing. I bet on her. Recently, I encountered her in Tyler, Texas, where she is a leader in the community and married to Judge Harry Loftis. A mother of three children and a lover of books, Margaret Ann Loftis reorganized the libraries in Tyler, doing such an outstanding job that the Ford Foundation provided the funds for her to improve other libraries.

"You made it all possible," she said.

Another of my winners was Malcolm Kutner, who became one of the greatest All-American ends the University of Texas has ever produced. Our association continued for years after his graduation and a hitch with the Chicago Cardinals pro football team. He worked for me in the oil fields as a scout, then as a geologist and took a law course at Tyler while still working for me. He's on his own now, in Houston, and doing well with his own company.

I didn't automatically give up on someone who failed to finish college. There was this linebacker who was booted out for cheating. He got himself a job selling beer. When he came to see me about his loan, I told him, "Get out of this beer racket and find yourself a respectable job."

Surprisingly, he followed the advice, quit running around, got married, and is doing fine.

In two cases, I shored up the school's athletic fortunes, with Leon Black, who became basketball coach after graduation, and track coach Cleburne Price.

All my contributions were on the up-and-up, but I must admit to a prejudice in favor of those who engaged in varsity sports. Ninety percent of the money I advanced went to athletes.

As far as I was concerned, nothing was too good for the Longhorns. For instance, when Texas won an Orange Bowl game, I invited the team to a celebration at the best night club in Miami, along with their dates, the queens and their maidens from the Orange Bowl Parade.

In no time, with the girls sparkling, the beer flowing and the vicissitudes of a tough season behind them, those athletes were blowing the lid off with a thunderous version of "The Eyes of Texas Are Upon You." The maitre d'hotel hurried up to me in horror.

"Monsieur is the host?" he asked. I nodded. "Please, the *noise*. We have other guests. I ask your consideration."

"If they want to blow off a little steam," I answered, "let 'em. They've earned it."

He walked off with a pained expression. Meanwhile, the vocalizing increased and the man was soon back, mustache quivering.

"The noise is impossible," he said. "The singing must stop. At once!"

I asked to see the owner, who was duly summoned.

"I'm here representing Beaufort Jester, governor of Texas. This is a winning team and I want them to have a good time, including the singing of 'The Eyes of Texas.' I'm willing to spend $7500 on a party. Do you want us to stay?"

"Yes, *sir*," he said.

"Then send this dude home."

He turned to the headwaiter and gave a jerk of his thumb.

"You heard what the man said," he told him. With the departure of the head waiter, we took over and had ourselves a whale of a time.

Before I leave the subject of my love affair with The University of Texas, there's a little more to be said about its marching band, of which I became honorary president and the dispenser of watches for excellent musicianship.

I had taken an interest in a musically gifted Englishman, Colonel Hurt, and persuaded him to organize a small band at a high school in Dallas. When the band won two national championships in a row, I and my geologist friend Bob Whitehead had no trouble landing Hurt a job at the University. Hurt was succeeded after his death by one Vince Di Nino. Why not, I asked myself, get the new band conductor off to a flying start with the world's biggest drum? I'd heard about the great drum they had at the University of Chicago, which had been gathering dust in a basement after Chicago gave up football.

Preliminary investigation revealed that we were trying to acquire a radioactive instrument. It had been stored in the same basement used by Enrico Fermi in splitting the atom for the Manhattan Project, which terminated World War II at Hiroshima. So first off, we had to destroy the drumhead. Then we tracked down an eighty-three-year-old man named Greenleaf, who had built the drum in 1921.

"I hear you've come up with the largest drum in the world and it's only right that we fix it up and send it to the largest school in the largest state in the Union," I told him. (This was true until Alaska was admitted to the Union, but Texas would still be the largest state if Alaska was ever melted down to size.)

Finding a hide large enough for the drumhead, which measured seventy-eight inches across, was another headache. Even the Armour meat packing company had nothing big enough, so we had to send them a cow from Texas.

It takes a crew of five to man the drum—four to haul it on its carriage, and one to beat it.

Taking a swat at "Big Bertha," the largest drum in the world, which I donated to the University of Texas band.

DHB

You might describe it as a whirlwind courtship—eight years, that is—before I got the bride to the altar. When Mattie (Martha) Caruth and I met in 1926, she was a Dallas socialite and heiress to 3,000 acres strategically situated within the city limits, plus another 3,600 acres outside. The story, for which I do not vouch, is that her forebears, who started out as merchants, turned to real estate when they discovered that they could trade a barrel of whiskey for a section (640 acres) of land.

The last thing I wanted was to "crash" Dallas society by marrying money, not that this would necessarily work; in Dallas, if you're not "in" you're "out." In any case, it was unnecessary, since my cousin Esiloy Wagoner was president of a social club, and his sister was a good friend of Mattie's. I was bound and determined to be on an equal financial footing before popping the question to her father, and during our married years I have never used any of her money for my business ventures.

Life was good for a bachelor, living with a group of gay blades at the Dallas Athletic Club, and I was in no haste to end my freedom. Bess Bond, later my secretary, was on the switchboard at the time and says that she had to complete an early course in diplomacy while she juggled telephone calls from females from various parts of the country.

Along with this, I saw Mattie with increasing frequency at parties and cultural functions and gradually made inroads on her defenses. We had a great deal in common besides money and dancing, at which she was of championship caliber. We were in solid agreement on how to use money, including generosity toward the church. We were both religious.

I finally approached her father, with whom I had come to enjoy a warm relationship; mothers had never posed any problem since I had learned early that if you court the mother, the daughter is usually a cinch.

"If you can stand her," Mr. Caruth replied forthrightly, "you can jolly well have her."

We were married on June 8, 1935, and embarked on virtually a three-year honeymoon of almost constant travel, beginning with a trip to Hawaii. In due course, Mattie presented me with two fine sons: David Harold Byrd, Jr., born in 1937, and Caruth Clark Byrd in 1941, both of whom have proved to be a blessing (at times a mixed blessing) and have warmed the cockles of my old heart with grandchildren.

While we were vacationing in Europe, I had a close-up preview of Adolph Hitler's military buildup, particularly in air power, and began to feel the chill of an approaching World War into which the United States must be inevitably drawn. There was no question in my mind but that our own woefully neglected posture in aviation would need a tremendous boost. My previous interest in all phases of aviation assumed a new and grimmer purpose.

Back home in Dallas, I began my own campaign to help get the country ready in time, concurrently with my multifarious business and civic activities. Often they intermingled in a cross-pollination that was good for Dallas, as well as for the country.

Chapter Six

Texas Goes to War

Another American who came back from his trips to Europe with a story to tell about the resurgence of military aviation under Hitler and Goering was Charles A. Lindbergh. He sincerely believed that the Third Reich could quickly win a blitzkrieg strike against the western European democracies and bomb out England in the bargain.

As the leader of the "America First" isolationists, the Lone Eagle passionately appealed to his countrymen to stay completely aloof from any involvement. Thus, he incurred the wrath of President Roosevelt, who was following an opposite policy and believed that a commissioned Air Corps reserve officer should fall in line. Roosevelt revoked Lindbergh's commission, although he eventually reinstated him as a civilian adviser after war broke out. Lindbergh then loyally contributed valuable services to the United States, finding ways to greatly extend the range of our fighter aircraft and flying unofficial combat missions in the war against the Rising Sun of General Tojo.

I agreed with Lindbergh's assessment of the threat represented by Hitler's new Luftwaffe. However, my close friend, Ernst Udet, who was on an intimate basis with many American pilots because of his exploits in the Cleveland Air Races between the two World Wars, but who was now a highly placed official in the Luftwaffe, held a minority opinion.

"You guys are going to win," he said flatly. "The Führer is building an air force to support the ground forces, but he just doesn't understand the true use of air power, like 'Tooey' Spaatz and Eaker. You're going to knock our ears off."

For my part, I preached to anyone who would listen. My conviction was that the United States had better get off its butt and start preparing for the worst—by no means a popular position to take in 1938.

One who listened was Governor Allred, who appointed me to the Texas Civil Aeronautics Commission.

From this vantage point, I joined with other Texans in an exhaustive survey of our airports. Air Corps and Navy surveys had previously given Texas a high rating for flyable weather year round and for flat terrain in most of the state. Flying cadets from Randolph and Kelly Fields forced down by weather or engine failure used to say that they could close their eyes and land safely almost anywhere without encountering any obstacle more formidable than a cow or a clump of mesquite trees.

I certainly saw no exaggeration in the aspiration of Dallas to become known as "The Crossroads of Aviation" in America. So, I began bombarding Texas congressmen in Washington and Admiral Chester Nimitz with correspondence touting Dallas as the logical site for construction of a major naval air station for the mass training of aviators, if needed, and in any case to permit naval reserve aviators to maintain their proficiency when off active duty. Otherwise, a large contingent of flyers in the Dallas area would be forced to range as far afield as Kansas City for the nearest reserve training facilities.

I got no support from Admiral Nimitz, but the Navy finally selected Hensley Field, midway between Dallas and Fort Worth alongside a large lake suitable for seaplanes, for the construction of the Dallas Naval Air Station. It would have the potential to train 1200 student pilots a year, subsequently a major contribution to the war effort.

Love Field, right in Dallas, had been my first choice. Nevertheless, I was well satisfied to see its runways and other facilities greatly improved by Lockheed Aircraft Company's decision to locate a major modification center there. It so happened that I was a good customer of Lockheed, having purchased the first Lockheed 12 off of their production line, to be followed by my acquisition of more Lodestars from Carl Squier, a vice-president of Lockheed.

DHB

Impaired eyesight, which had dogged me since my college days, stood in the way of my becoming a combat pilot, but there was an alternative—organize and take part in a "Civil Air Patrol."

So sound was the original concept of CAP, as it became known, that the organization flourishes to this day as an auxiliary of the United States Air Force, performing essential services in air searches, rescue work, and in all kinds of emergency situations. The idea, as formulated by pioneer aviator Gill Robb Wilson and me, on the back of a menu card while dining at the Peacock Terrace of the Baker Hotel in Dallas in September, 1941, was that a large potential of unused flying talent would go to waste, in the event of hostilities, unless those pilots who were too old or otherwise not qualified for military duty could be mobilized (Vic Beau, another champion of the CAP concept, became its first national commander). We all foresaw a crying need for civil pilots to perform antisub-

This uniform I'm wearing was the first Civil Air Patrol uniform, and is now in the Smithsonian Institute.

marine patrol, freeing military pilots for more pressing tasks, as indeed was to prove the case.

Two days after the Japanese wiped out most of our battleships concentrated at Ford Island, on December 7, 1941, a group of us Texans met in Washington and got CAP officially organized as an arm of civil defense, which was under the direction of Fiorello H. LaGuardia. My friend Tom Connally insisted that I assume command of the Texas wing and LaGuardia duly appointed me.

The whole country was in a state of jitters about possible attacks on our coasts from U-boats and Japanese aircraft carriers. If it could happen in Hawaii, why not in San Francisco or Los Angeles? The carrier threat never materialized, although in the ludicrous "Battle of Los Angeles," a false alarm triggered the valiant defenders into a nightlong barrage of antiaircraft fire, supported by weaving searchlights, against a sky that proved to be free of enemy aircraft.

German U-boats were a far more serious matter.

Submarines immediately began wreaking a heavy toll of shipping in the sea lanes near our coasts and in attacks on our convoys. Oil tankers, in particular, were being sent to the bottom at an alarming rate within sight of the Statue of Liberty and elsewhere along the Atlantic Coast and in the Gulf of Mexico.

Civilian volunteer pilots rushed to join CAP, bringing their own planes, radios, and repair equipment to hastily improvised bases to operate against the U-boats. I assumed personal command of the antisubmarine base at Beaumont, Texas, and was in the thick of it.

The experimental CAP, brought into existence on a ninety-day trial basis, proved so successful that bases were set up along the entire East Coast and the Gulf, flying missions around the clock.

Altogether, I donated nine aircraft to the cause, five of which were lost.

Submarines about to attack convoys crash dived on the approach of CAP aircraft, although the land planes, mostly single-engined, were entirely unarmed. But if you were a U-boat captain, how could you be sure? Later, bombs and depth charges were added with deadly effect. CAP pilots with an observer, in which capacity I flew many missions, eventually flew more than 24 million miles over the ocean, spotted 173 submarines, attacked 57, and sank a confirmed two, in addition to those sunk by military aircraft summoned to the scene by radio from CAP planes.

The sharp eyes of CAP observers were responsible for the survival of 363 victims of ship sinkings or aircraft ditchings and spotted seventeen floating mines, often lying in the path of approaching troop ships. Altogether, twenty CAP members lost their lives in forced landings at sea and six in crashes on land. Seven were seriously injured and a total of ninety planes were lost or damaged beyond repair.

Measured on the scale of a global war, all this may seem to be small potatoes, but I will always be proud of having been able to play a role in the Civil Air Patrol. I remained an active member long after the war, opposing its disbandment and persuading General Tooey Spaatz to become the first board chairman of a permanent organization.

I launched the CAP cadet movement, and a cadet foreign exchange program, among other things, to keep alive a public awareness of the importance of maintaining strong air power in America after the cessation of hostilities.

The fact that in many quarters I became known as "Mr. CAP" helped me to feel that I had not done badly in my all-out, day-and-night effort to organize, train, and direct the operations of the Texas contingent of CAP and to do all in my power to gain them the recognition they earned.

DHB

A vital question for America when war began was oil and how to transport it from the rich fields in Texas to the East Coast refineries in the quantities that would suffice to meet the insatiable appetite of tanks, ships, aircraft, submarines, and almost every other piece of equipment without which no modern fighting machine could function.

The answers were the "Big Inch" and the "Little Inch" pipelines, twenty-four inches and twenty inches in diameter, respectively. The first part of the story is not a pretty one. Although as early as 1939, when Hitler invaded Poland, the head of the Texas Railroad Commission, Ernest O. Thompson, had begged President Roosevelt to build pipelines to the East in order to free our tanker fleet for the transportation of petroleum products to the war zones, he was ignored. Isolationists called him an "alarmist." Glenn McCarthy strongly advocated the pipelines as did Harold L. Ickes, Secretary of the Interior, who predicted that they would prove to be "absolutely necessary" in the event of war. For one thing, they would be sinkproof.

It remained for the wise leaders of seven major oil companies to join forces in plans to build the Big Inch with their own resources, organizing National Defense Pipelines with $80 million of working capital. Yet, twice, their application for a priority for steel was rejected. Granted, a hell of a lot of steel was involved. So, it was not until the Japanese forced us into the war that the priority was finally authorized.

So much for the blindness in Washington. Once the consortium of oil companies was given the green light, the two pipelines were constructed at a breakneck pace over the 1400 miles that separated Texas from the elaborate refinery facilities near New York City and Philadelphia. The Little Inch followed a course from Beaumont, Texas, to a link-up with the Big Inch near Little Rock, Arkansas, then paralleled it the rest of the way.

Completed at the war's height in 1943, the Big Inch began delivering nearly 300,000 barrels of crude oil daily, and the Little Inch close to 200,000 barrels. The significance of these figures is apparent when it is recalled that *six days* were required for a tanker to deliver only 100,000 barrels from the Gulf, exposed to ocean hazards.

Another farsighted action taken by Texans, sparked by Commissioner Thompson, was a measure to provide insurance against a wasteful drain of the Texas oil fields. The problem was that if you didn't pump enough salt water back into the wells, there would not be enough pressure to force the oil to the surface. Huge quantities of oil would have remained in the ground as a total loss. So an "allowable" limit was placed on the amount of oil you could produce, geared to the amount of salt water you pumped back into the field.

Here was an example of regulation, at the state level, with which I cannot quarrel, meeting as it did an overriding consideration. Likewise, I had no quarrel with wartime price controls, although I estimate that they cost me millions of dollars.

It has been the postwar price controls which I deplore, wiping out, as they do, the incentive of the independents to find new oil. I know that this smacks of a tired cliché but you just plain can't have the necessary incentives without a free market pricing system.

When will we learn that nobody is interested in risking money on the hope of maybe breaking even?

If the reader will indulge me in yet another chauvinistic blast, I look back on those war years with the conviction that the Lone Star State did itself proud. They did it with the Civil Air Patrol. They did it by building the Big Inch and the Little Inch. They did it by the timely actions of state authorities to conserve the country's supply of oil. And they did it through the example of Texans who served as airmen, sailors, and Marines, and lowly dogfaces, wherever the fighting was the fiercest.

So we got the job done and finally, with other Texas free enterprisers, I could turn my attention once more to the exciting business of making a buck.

Chapter Seven

Diversification and Crisis

Your free enterpriser, in addition to his penchant for bold risk taking, often displays an amazing capacity for diversification. My postwar years confirm that I was surely guilty of one of these. I spread myself all over Texas and beyond, and the variety of my interests would make a single-minded individual shudder.

I was either in a management position, or held a heavy interest in the following: farming, ranching, feedlots, and hardware stores, trusts and foundations, financial and investment companies, residential and industrial real estate, recreational complexes, and a lot of "just-for-the-heck-of-it" ventures, over and above my primary operations in oil and gas.

I was an easy mark for anybody with a new idea, and I probably drove the more sedentary of my associates half crazy.

Given these conditions, my wife Mattie did an outstanding job of adapting. One reason I had married her was that she was the best dancer in Dallas—some said of professional quality. She never stepped on my toes when, for example, I'd call her up from the telephone in my car on my way home after seven in the evening and inform her that I had four guests and how about dinner in twenty minutes? If I decided on the spur of the moment to take a trip to Europe, Mattie was fortunate to receive any more of a warning than "Come on, Mattie, let's go."

Rather than bore you with a blow-by-blow account of all my endeavors during the 1950s and to date, I'll try to touch only on some of the high spots. And some hair-raising lows. Twice I was to go nearly bankrupt.

DHB

A real high point for me was the 8535-foot elevation at which I brought in a gas well in 1952 at Clear Lake, east of Salt Lake City, on the Continental Divide, the highest well in the world. From there I'd next have to construct a 118-mile long pipe line that would provide low-cost heating for the first time to the 6,000 homes in the state capital which were adaptable to gas for heating.

The venture, my first big move in the oil business so far afield from Texas, had begun with leases of a million acres (at 25¢ an acre) from the Indians and state and federal agencies in the Four Corners region, where Utah, Colorado, New Mexico, and Arizona are contiguous.

I put my airplane to good use in scouting the mountainous terrain, looking for promising geological structures. Incidentally, I've always felt that if an airplane didn't pay for itself in one year, in terms of time saved, and in the edge it gave a free enterpriser in exploiting opportunities where hours or even minutes counted, there was something wrong either with the owner or the business he was in.

My first set of aerial photos was confusing when checked against my geological surveys, for the shadows at different hours of the day gave a badly distorted picture. Therefore, I had to repeat the survey of the 2500 square miles, after which I located twenty structures and drilled eight wells, six of which brought in fields over an extended period in the 1950s.

Artist's conception of rig and works of Winkler County discovery well that has meant so many millions of dollars to the University of Texas.

It was a time when my talents as a negotiator were tested to the limit in a long drawn-out struggle for position in the formation of a new company, Three States Natural Gas Company, to exploit both the pipeline and natural gas possibilities from El Paso to Los Angeles as well as the proposed pipeline to Salt Lake City. I had reached the major decision to divest my holdings in Byrd-Frost, Inc., and exchange them for a strong position in the new Three States Natural Gas Company, as an individual stockholder. The resulting maneuverings brought me into contact with a colorful cast of strong-minded characters such as Jock Whitney, whom I persuaded to put in $1 million dollars, Fred Anderson, a retired Air Force general, Paul Kaiser, head of El Paso Natural Gas Company, P.B. English, John McGuire, Max Cohen, Clint Murchison, and Glenn Turner.

Clint Murchison came out on top in the maneuvering for the lucrative El Paso-Los Angeles pipeline, after Kaiser double-crossed me, but I got even with Kaiser later, as I shall relate, on the pipeline to Salt Lake City.

Utah, like other states, had a commission that ruled on the feasibility of such matters as pipelines and the capacity of ours to deliver 136 million cubic feet of gas per day. A hearing was duly held, with competitors Clint Murchison and Glenn Turner denigrating my application with the argument that my well would never meet the daily quota, whereas their source of gas was more than ample.

Representatives of the coal industry testified that a gas line would confront them with ruinous competition. Petroleum engineers took the floor for Murchison, armed with impressive credentials. The lines were drawn.

During a recess, I huddled with my attorney to plan a counterstrategy. We decided to acknowledge and emphasize the qualifications of the chief geologist of the opposition, as a psychological ploy to hoist him by his own petard. After we'd built him up, our cross-examination went approximately like this:

"How many fields have you brought in, sir?"

"One."

Next we questioned Glenn Turner:

"Are you prepared to invest the $5 million needed to lay this line?"

"Well, first," he answered, "I'd have to bring the matter before our board of directors for the authorization."

Now I took the stand and was asked, "How many oil and gas fields have you brought in?"

"Oh, I guess a couple of dozen—maybe six to eight in this immediate vicinity."

"Would you commit $5 million to this project?"

"I would."

"Do you have the company books that authorize you to do this?"

"I don't carry my books around with me."

"What about an authorization from your shareholders?"

"I don't have it. But if you'll give me a moment, I'll get it." I glanced across the room at my partner Jack Frost.

"Okay with you, Jack?"

"Okay," he said.

Then I turned to my secretary-treasurer, Miss Margaret Clark, who owned exactly two shares. She allowed that it was fine with her, too. I faced my questioner.

"I have the approval of a majority of our stockholders," I concluded. "We are authorized to spend the money."

With little further ado we were granted permission to proceed with the pipeline.

Subsequently, I evened the score with Kaiser, when he decided that El Paso Natural Gas wanted to buy me out.

"It will cost you double," I told him.

We made a profit of four to one.

When all the smoke had cleared, an auditor would have been hard pressed to tell me where I stood following a multitude of transactions during the transfer of my holdings in Byrd-Frost, Inc., to the new company. All I know is that my income was often close to half a million a month, and that there were two years in a row that I paid more than $1 million in taxes to the government.

In my main objective I had failed. I had started out aiming to retire, to cash in on my Byrd-Frost holdings and leave the daily operating headaches to the management of the new Three States Natural Gas Company. I wasn't the first to discover the difficulties, if not the near impossibility, of just walking away. The easy-going policies of the new management, plus mismanagement, gave me great concern. As a stockholder and, at first, a member of the board of directors, I no longer had the "muscle" to control my own destiny.

Dear friends of mine, Warren and Mary Wagner, are facing a similar problem today in escaping from the rat race, but for a different reason. Starting from scratch, Wagner became a successful farmer and the "spinach king" of Crystal City, accumulating $7 million. He's figured that he could retire with some $30,000 coming in every month, but there's a hitch. He simply wouldn't know what to do with himself for the rest of his life. He's a voracious reader, but you can't just read books. So he keeps on plugging away at a game he has already won.

It may be worth mentioning that my impatience with the old saw that nobody does anything about the weather got me into the air-conditioning business in its infancy.

If you've ever arrived at Dallas-Fort Worth International Airport, stepped from an air-conditioned airliner into an air-conditioned terminal, transferred to an air-conditioned taxicab to an air-conditioned office building for a meeting, to an air-conditioned restaurant for the businessman's lunch of two glasses of white wine, to an air-conditioned hotel or motel or private residence, then entertain a kindly passing thought for Dry Hole Byrd. I not only dehumidified the state of Texas, I practically froze it, through acquisition of an early patent.

In the mid-1930s, I air-conditioned the first private home and the first office building in Dallas and went on from there to cool down twenty-five other structures, before Chrysler Corporation got into the act, disputing my patent. The air-conditioning of America, and the nation's automobiles, followed much later.

You can chalk this off to the tendency of the entrepreneur to get mixed up in anything that addresses itself to the question, "What's new, Mac?"

DHB

As of this writing, I am still smarting from the licking I have taken on an investment in Mexico.

The story goes a long way back, to 1926, when I was approached in San Antonio by a Mexican acquaintance from the University of Texas, Ramon Munoz, and his partner Fidel Martinez, both petroleum engineers, about an oil venture near Mier, in Old Mexico. (At one time, Mier was the capital of Texas). Both had married into wealthy families in Monterrey, Mexico, where Martinez's wife owned a large brewery; after she was admitted to a mental institution, he assumed responsibilities for her estate.

Munoz and Martinez had obtained an option to lease the oil rights on a well-defined geological structure, the Solado Arch, which had been expropriated by the Mexican government. They wanted me to join forces as their agent to raise capital. I agreed to go to New York City and scare up the money. Accordingly, I phoned the president of Dixie Oil Company, asking him to come to New York, all expenses paid if a deal materialized.

We met with a representative of Standard Oil of Indiana, and I made my presentation, neglecting to mention that I was subsisting on a diet of five-cent apples from the fruit stands that abounded during the Depression. There was initial resistance to the size of the royalty fee I wanted, so we compromised and came up with a deal which gave me and my Mexican partners $186,000, split three ways. It was sufficient to start them in business and operate for seven years before they came to me again for increased financing.

This time, they needed money to build a pipeline from McAllen, Texas, to Monterrey, Mexico, a distance of a hundred miles. Having arrived at the status of a major independent in 1934, I was in a position to put up the money with the help of Moody-Seagraves, which was to provide for construction of a brewery and a glass factory, as well as the pipeline, in which I reserved 20% "space" for myself.

While flying near Mier, my attention was grabbed by a geological structure that appeared to be loaded with possibilities. I immediately photographed it, then had Munoz and Martinez confirm my hunch, on the ground, with a geological map. We leased 72,000 acres in all before I had even set foot on the properties, to select a location for the fourth well, the first three having already come in gushers. We continued drilling until we had brought in a total of eight.

For something like twenty years, I continued to plow back Byrd-Frost's share of earnings into development of new industries in Monterrey. The glass factory we built, with 8600 employees, became the largest on the North American continent. I increased my Mexican investments, leasing up barite strata, eighteen feet thick. Barite was basic to the manufacture of paint and "mixing mud," to keep the drill stem from sticking. Neil Mallon, now head of Dresser Industries, built my barite plant and became our big customer for barite, providing us with a good market for years.

So far, so good. Then the trouble started. The President of Mexico abruptly ordered the expropriation of the Munoz-Martinez property, with the proviso, however, that I would be adequately compensated for the improvements I had contributed over the years.

To this day, no such adjustment has been forthcoming. In fact, Mexico eventually repudiated the entire agreement on the technical grounds that the stock held by the three of us was not required to bear the owners' names. Meanwhile, I have received no payments of any kind; offset drilling is going on all around the property, draining its reserves; deals are being made without my knowledge or approval; and I am no longer a factor in the estimated trillion feet of gas, and a billion barrels of oil, seized in the takeover.

I asked my lawyer to go down there and protect my interests, but he refused with the plea, "What, and get myself bumped off?" I had to engage a Monterrey lawyer, who was promptly bought off and wound up refusing to acknowledge my interests. Munoz, who died before the expropriation, was never to my knowledge a double-crosser, but Martinez, after we had been partners for seven years definitely turned liar and thief.

As a last resort, I flew to the Johnson Ranch and asked L.B., an old friend, if there weren't *some* protection for a private American investor in Mexico. Surprisingly, he confessed that there was no way that even the President of the United States could intervene. Through some kind of understanding between the Mexican and United States governments, I had no recourse at the diplomatic level in a private dispute over ownership.

"Don't even tell me the name of the property," Johnson said.

And so the matter stands.

From my own experience with the Mexicans, I would generalize that the peons, the workers, like us and are grateful for the jobs and benefits that stem from the investment of American capital in their country. It is the upper class that resents the "Gringo Exploiter," who reaps profits that are taken out of the country. No matter, it seems that profits are shared and that there would be no profits in the first place unless some enterpriser had started the ball rolling.

DHB

The repudiation of my large investments in Mexico was bad enough. But worse was to come. At the very time that I could least afford it, I found myself in a bind with payments of $30,000 per month in development costs for a marina called "Newport Dunes," a recreational complex for which I was responsible in Newport Beach, California. Simultaneously, I was the victim of an antitrust suit brought by the federal government against booming Ling-Temco-Vought, in which I was, and still am, a heavy stockholder, virtually pulling the rug out from under me.

Here is how it happened.

I was one of the original investors in Temco Aircraft Corporation. It grew and prospered until it occupied plants at Dallas, Garland, and Greenville, Texas. I decided that we were ready for bigger things and liked the idea of bringing more "glamor" to our line of aviation-oriented products through a merger with my friend Jim Ling, who was making great strides with his electronics company.

I've always regarded Ling as a brilliant businessman, and sure enough, he proved himself a hard bargainer in the proposed exchange of stock. When I agreed to place his name first in the new company, Ling-Temco became a reality. A year later, in 1961, Ling-Temco, in turn, absorbed the Chance Vought Corporation, a blue-chip aircraft manufacturer, with its famous line of Corsairs for the Navy. Ling-Temco-Vought became a formidable presence in the aerospace business.

Diversifying further, we made one more acquisition—Jones & Laughlin Steel Company. This set off a knee-jerk reaction in the Department of Justice, which claimed that we were getting too "big."

Now I've never been able to understand why getting too "big" is a sin. Big jobs require big companies. General Motors, for example, has grown enormously by any standards, but the public has foolproof protection against the danger of "monopoly." If they don't like the set-up, all they have to do is stop buying General Motors' cars and throw their business to smaller competitors.

Under the ominous cloud of the antitrust suit, LTV stock reacted downward. The profits of Jones & Laughlin, about $65 million before the acquisition, reversed themselves into an annual *loss* of nearly the same amount in one year's time.

My LTV stock, pledged at the bank as collateral for loans to finance my Newport Dunes and other investments, shrank from a high selling price of 168 down to 12. We eventually won the antitrust suit, but the damage had been done, after self-serving actions behind the scenes in some company board rooms had occurred.

Within two months, I absorbed a loss on paper of around $15 million, while my commitments at Newport Dunes drained me white. I had to meet the monthly costs of building a marina, the "Seabyrd Restaurant" at $680,000, a trailer park, and the overhead of twenty-five regular employees, plus security guards, offices, and other expenses.

What was tying my hands was that there seemed no way for me to secure a clear title, under California law, to my Newport property. In the mean time, the money to keep going had to come out of my own pocket. After negotiating with some local people, among them William T. Evans of San Diego, and Haige C. Merrigan of La Jolla, I disposed of 80% of my interest. Without doing this, I doubt that I could have held out six months longer.

I have to say, without going into detail, that my experience with the Californians was not a happy one.

My resources had been strained to the limit by a double blow from the wheel of fortune, and if the Mexican confiscation is included, a triple whammy.

But I am proud to say that, today, I am still afloat.

Chapter Eight

Looking Back

It is late in the year 1977, and I am engaged in a Saturday morning chore which I enjoy, because my thoughts have a chance to roam. I am riding a power mower, cutting the grass at my three-acre residence on Vassar Drive in Dallas, where I have spent the past forty-four years.

The sun shines hot and the birds are calling sporadically—grackles, mockingbirds, crows, blackbirds, and redbirds—from the two huge pecan trees that shade the house. At nightfall, the scenery will come alive with the orchestration of millions of locusts and crickets, like the roaring surf.

The two story house, of white brick, with its fifteen rooms, including a game room which was added on to form a wing by itself, stands there a solid symbol of security and a sanctuary in time of stress. A red-painted concrete driveway leads up to a large parking area and the main entrance, with the six-car garage for my Cadillacs in the rear. The tall front door seems to beckon guests, "Come on in, there's always room for one more."

I suppose, to the stranger, the house is an imposing sight, which indeed it was intended to be in my early days when I was dealing with impressionable New York bankers.

The interior is replete with artifacts gathered from all over the world, reflecting particularly Mattie's predilection for Oriental art. I imagine that the jade and ivory

(text continued on page 75)

The Byrd home at 6909 Vassar Drive, Dallas, Texas.

The "International Room" of my home. A collection made by Mattie and me in our travels all over the world.

My trophy room is more than just a large collection of animals I've hunted all over the world, it's a gallery of priceless memories.

carvings, the turquoise, the china, the gold, and the silver that we accumulated must be worth a fortune. Orientals, incidentally, prize jade more highly than gold.

We added a large wing to the house just to accommodate a large animal collection ranging from two huge polar bears to a Sumatran tiger, with all manner of African bovines staring from the walls, silent reminders of my safaris. (Caruth and I brought back from Africa fifteen specimens, including springbok, wildebeest, gemsbok, hartebeest, ostrich, impala, tcessabee, lechwe, kudu, and cape buffalo.) This trophy room serves also as a projection room.

We have a music room, which my younger son Caruth has put to good use as a skilled pianist, besides playing acceptably a total of fifteen instruments. Among other assailants, Van Cliburn and Jose Iturbi have crashed out their chords on the grand piano.

At the risk of damaging my image as an intrepid hunter, I should mention that I have a *doll* room, completely given over to a collection of foot-high dolls in native costume from all countries. It started innocently enough when I sent dolls purchased on my travels to one of my sisters, who was a hardcore doll lover. Soon I was hooked too.

I pause in my mowing to wipe my brow, and my mind wanders back to those years when we gave an annual party on the lawn after the Texas-Oklahoma game. We began with a couple of hundred guests, a total which swelled to eighteen hundred over the years. We made the mistake (if it was one) of encouraging people to "bring a friend" next time, so, like Topsy, she just grew. But if anyone failed to show up, they were never invited again.

From the beginning, two of our "regulars" were William W. Heath, our able ambassador to Sweden for many years, and his delightful wife, Mavis, who was to become my second wife, after Mattie died, although I scarcely suspected it at the time. My great admiration for Bill Heath

Mattie and I looking at my doll collection made during my travels all over the world.

overshadowed the presence of Mavis as part of a warm friendship. Only after I became a widower and she a widow did the lightning strike, of which more later. The Heaths usually brought with them from Austin a party of loyal Texas alumni, and their wives.

In memory, I can see again the swarms of guests feasting on barbecued steaks plus more exotic fare from the East African hunt, washed down with floods of beer and bourbon, and the dancing to the strains of "Deep in the Heart of Texas."

Our invitation lists included Presidents Truman and Johnson, governors, congressmen, and a host of celebrities, turning the chore of telephoning friends from all over America, like the Ed Pauleys in Los Angeles, into a major project begun weeks in advance.

One of the parties on the grounds of "The Country Place."

Mattie and I adhered to an iron rule not to indulge in alcohol at our own parties, or we never could have coped properly with the role of host and hostess. We found that you can get pretty "high" just on 100-proof friendship.

I recall one time when the bartenders were being temporarily swamped and one of our guests decided to earn his keep as a waiter. One lady accepted his refill, then stared at him closely.

"Excuse me," she said, "But you bear a remarkable resemblance to the governor of Texas."

"I *am* the governor," he replied, moving with his tray to the next group of guests. That was typical of my dear friend Buford Jester.

D.H. and Mattie Byrd watching Carol Burnett bowling at "The Country Place."

DHB

I am sitting in my upstairs den, kicking around a real estate deal on the phone with my lawyer. After I hang up, my eyes stray to a motto I had framed to hang on the wall:

"Great Sorrows Have Gigantic Power of Enlarging the Soul."

I have never recovered from the hurt of losing my father and my mother; the fact that their deaths were inevitable didn't help one bit to ease the suffering. And there was great pain, too, in the passing of others—close friends and relatives.

When Mattie, who had been at my side for 37 years, died of a long illness in 1972, I had to reach way down inside me for solace.

But the loneliness, especially when evening came, was intolerable—no one with whom to share the events of the day, a game of cards, or hold my hand for grace at dinner. We had had our differences. It was her idea to hire a male "governess" to help bring up our young sons, sparing me the role of stern parent, correcting their table manners and meting out appropriate punishments for sins of commission and omission.

I know that she was trying to ease the burden of my heavy responsibilities for all of the Byrd enterprises, and it is true that she couldn't very well say, "wait 'til your father gets home," when my schedule forced me into so many long absences. But I questioned whether hers was the right solution.

In the depths of my loneliness, I found myself turning more and more to Mavis, on my frequent trips to Austin. She was lonely too. My technique as a suitor was probably rusty, but perhaps by sheer persistence, I won her consent. First, though, in a complete switch from the traditional paternal role, I sought, and obtained, the consent of both my sons and Mavis' two daughters for the marriage.

And there is another motto which I have framed and think about often: "Happiness is Having Something to Do, Something to Look Forward to, and Someone to Love."

I still have a host of things to do and to look forward to, like any other man who keeps busy. And I still have someone to love. Mavis has taken care of that department. What made an indelible impression on me during our courtship was, for the want of any other word, her *guts*. She had broken her hip just before we took a trip with friends and was suffering excruciating pain. You'd never have known it, though, by her stoicism and good spirits. I said to myself, "Grab her while you can. If she can be that good a sport, maybe she can even put up with you."

Mavis has a penchant for criticizing me often and severely, and if there's one thing I can't take gracefully, it's unsolicited criticism. But two people who have a lifetime of living under their belts are bound to have acquired some characteristics which are too late to change. I find her exasperating, but irresistible. That's enough. And I love it.

Literally, a second life has opened up to me, thanks to Mavis' two vivacious daughters, her three granddaughters, and two grandsons, all of whom have accepted me affectionately as "Papa Byrd." Her daughters are Linda Heath of Dallas, who, in January 1978, married Schuler Nelson, and Cynthia Heath, who married Dewey Ray of Big Springs (their daughter, Hanna, married Dr.

Phil Overton of Austin). They have been a godsend to an old fud like me who might otherwise have given up hope of ever again warming his hands at the glowing hearth of a close-knit family.

DHB

I identified with, and suffered acutely from, the growing-up ordeals of my sons, Harold and Caruth, but both boys found themselves in manhood. I like to recall the time when young Harold went off to college and I gave him a stake of $3000 beyond college expenses as a present. Instead of frittering the money away on self-indulgences, Harold sought some good advice, invested wisely, and in due course startled me with the news that his original $3000 had sprouted into $30,000.

Younger brother Caruth, your typical extrovert, always good company (whereas Harold is more the introvert), exhibited a wild streak that he has tamed with the passage of time. As a successful motion picture and TV producer, he may yet wind up with more money than the conservative Harold, who goes in for real estate ventures. Both sons were independent enough of mind not to follow their old man into the oil business.

Appearing on a TV show featuring ten prominent young Texans who had made their mark relatively early, Caruth was preceded by several self-made millionaires. Thus, when his turn came, he was asked, "And you, sir, tell us how you made your first million."

"I inherited it," Caruth replied, "from my mother."

DHB

I think gratefully of my good fortune in having had the services, at the vortex of my often turbulent affairs, of Bess Bond, nominally my private secretary for twenty-five years. I say "nominally" because she was much more than that. Gifted with a remarkable memory and a truly legal mind, she came to know more about me, in managing my personal and business affairs, than I know myself.

She was absolutely honest, loyal, and always fair, wielding the power of approval or rejection on all financial matters. It was she who once spotted an obscure typographical error in a complicated financial document that amounted to *one million dollars*. It sounds impossible, but batteries of lawyers and bankers had let the error slip by undetected. That's the kind of fanatical thoroughness I came to take for granted in Bess. Inevitably, she served also as an officer of my companies.

It took a very serious illness to force Bess into retirement. She now lives not far from me in Dallas and still complains that she misses the hubbub of operating "in Grand Central Station" at my downtown offices, and of being told, without warning, at 9:30 a.m., "Bess you're going to Los Angeles. Your plane leaves at eleven. Pack enough things for four days."

Whenever I'm tempted to feel sorry for myself after some cruel blow of fate, I need only recall that in the space of one year, recently, Bess lost six close relatives, including the sister who had kept house for her, making it a warm and loving home through the years, and, though far from being in good health herself, Bess managed to attend to all the details of settling their estates. During this, she paid daily visits to a brother critically ill in the hospital.

If that isn't indomitable courage, I don't know where you'll find it. Through it all, she has never lost her native warmth, charm, and optimism.

DHB

There have been low points, when things weren't going well, when I have been hard-pressed to wear a smile. But I have found that great sorrows and adversities apparently serve a purpose. They are a purgative. They cleanse you. Overall, they have reinforced my Christian faith in a meaning to life. If you'd never known suffering, what contrast would you have by which to measure joy or the thrill of achievement?

One thing seems certain. With our five limited senses, every one of us is vastly ignorant of the great mysteries that move silently around us. What is electricity? What is gravity? What is time? What is conscience, or for that matter, consciousness? What is courage? Does the wisest man who ever lived have the answers?

What is good or bad for us can be deceptive, as is dramatically illustrated in the case of a wild deer, swimming frantically out to sea towards sure death by drowning, striving desperately to elude the efforts of game wardens in a launch who are trying to haul it aboard and save its life. There is no way they can get it through the head of the terror-stricken animal that they are its friend. So it may be also with humans, unable to divine the purpose of so many of the forces that threaten us. Or seem to.

Let us accept the fact that what man has learned, in what amounts to the blink of an eye on history's time scale, impressive though it is in the age of television and space travel, merely places him closer to discoveries about himself that will some day come as a blinding light of revelation.

We are coming closer every passing day to some real answers. Someone, in a stumbling search for the secret panel, is going to touch the right button.

That is my religion.

Chapter Nine

A View from the Bridge

In my capacity as President of the Independent Petroleum Association of Texas, I have been asked, "How far down the road toward socialism do you think America has moved?"

If socialism is defined as "the elimination of private ownership of the means of production and distribution," (*Webster's Dictionary*), and if *regulation* of those means is construed as perilously close to "ownership," then I have to answer, "At least 60% of the way."

The communist countries have, of course, already moved nearly but not all of the way, while England, source of our political beliefs and our Bill of Rights, has moved perilously close to full socialism. Like American socialists (and the present Congress), they stubbornly prescribe, "The more harmful the medicine, the bigger the dose."

What then are the prospects that America can resist the global tide and retain what remains of its original commitment to the concept of free enterprise, in a political system where the best government has traditionally been the *least* government?

It is with the deepest reluctance that I confess my total disillusionment with the current trend of events. It strikes me that every major step being taken by the Carter administration—economic, fiscal, military, and international—is a stride further away from the system that made us the greatest nation in history, in terms of the general welfare of its citizens and of those who still risk life itself to escape to our shores and share the human rights which they could not find in their own lands.

Economically, the government each day applies new restraints on our freedoms in order to carry out an alien philosophy of doing good with other people's money, that is, the government's idea of what is "good" for you, not necessarily yours. It continues trying to solve our petroleum shortages by ignoring the only solution that will work, namely, "hands off."

Fiscally, the government seems committed to printing the money needed to carry out its programs—the oldest fallacy in human experience, invariably disastrous.

Militarily, we have embraced a new, though not yet officially announced, policy of one-sided reduction of our defense posture, hoping that the Soviet Union will follow suit, thus far in vain.

Internationally, our policy appears to have been drawn up with the object of bringing wreaths of smiles to the faces of the socialist planners in Moscow and Peking. We are writing a blueprint upon which they could scarcely have improved had they composed it themselves. When I say this, I am thinking of Cuba, Panama, Taiwan, South Korea, Africa, the Middle East, and Asia.

The more I think about it, the stranger it seems to me that we have elected a Congress and an administration that are hell-bent on "throwing" the fight to the socialist side. But then I find myself grasping at straws of hope, like the surprising selection of arch-conservative Milton Friedman as the winner of the 1977 Nobel Prize for Economics. Mr. Friedman, as a champion of the free market and sound monetary policy, is far out of step with most of his fellow economists. He asks, in effect, "When will we wake up and stop biting the hand that has fed us so long and so bountifully?"

I join with him wholeheartedly in the prayer that Americans will indeed wake up and act to preserve that marvelous mechanism, free enterprise, which proved to be so virile at the close of World War II that it was able to rebound from four years of the costliest war ever fought and extend a hand to its fallen foes and pull them back to their feet, as we did for all of Europe under the Marshall Plan. Japan and West Germany emulated our now-threatened example of productivity and sound money, as did little Free China on Taiwan, which has set postwar records for annual increases in its gross national product by glaring contrast with mainland China. The United States, of course, attained new heights of postwar prosperity, also. It is surely unique in history that defeated enemies have achieved such miraculous recoveries by borrowing a leaf out of the victor's original notebook, as well as a buck from his treasury.

England, alas, having followed the downhill road to socialism, now finds itself pinning its last hopes for economic survival on the accident of the North Sea oil discoveries to bail her out, yet, her labor leaders still cry shrilly for more, and inflation be damned.

Communism's great advantage over the Free World has been its ability to make arbitrary decisions at the top, and make them stick with no back talk. A recent example is the news from China that it has been able to cut its population explosion in half in just ten years—by decree. A couple is permitted to conceive two children and that's it.

If you agree that the world's four greatest problem areas are overpopulation, inflation, the existence of "the bomb," and pollution or mismanagement of our earthly resources, then all four problems may have to be met in the end by arbitrary decisions as drastic as China's approach to its population explosion. That is the trend, as I see it. I pray with all my heart that Americans can find a better way, as did our forebears in 1776, to ensure that freedom shall not perish from the earth. That is still my hope.

The Good Lord has seen fit to spare my life so many times when it might have been snuffed out that I often wonder if there has been a reason. I have refused to fly in bad weather when others, faced with the same conditions, took off anyway, crashed and were killed. Conversely, I have elected to fly when the birds were walking, and I always landed safely. Some uncanny instinct always guided me. Ace pilot Roscoe Turner once neglected to perform a routine preflight inspection on the aircraft in which he was flying me to Dallas. Sure enough, the engine conked out on final approach and we wound up in a spectacular crackup. Looking at the wreck, you wouldn't have believed it possible that we both escaped unhurt.

I think there was a reason for my many brushes with death, only to survive. I have been a *positive,* rather than a negative, force in living a life whose motto was: Make things happen. What are we waiting for? Let's do it now. Have the nerve to take chances.

It is true that I haven't always covered my rear. But isn't that to be expected? If you're too busy looking ahead?

Biographical Data On David Harold Byrd

I. Family Background

David Harold Byrd is descended from a branch of the famed Virginia Byrd family—and the son of pioneers. His father, Edward Byrd, was the grandson of the settlers who had pushed westward in 1799 into Missouri, while that state was still part of the Louisiana Territory. Edward was born at the Old Stone House (still standing) on Byrd's Creek, Byrd Township, Cape Girardeau County, Missouri. As a youth of nineteen, he came to Texas for the first time in 1873 in a covered wagon and stayed at Clarksville, in Lamar County, two months before returning to Missouri by pony, a trip that required a month. His next journey was by train, when he settled near Blossom, Lamar County. There in 1877 he joined the Presbyterian Church, became a ruling elder three weeks later, and subsequently represented his church at various times from the Red River Presbytery at the General Assembly.

He married in 1879 Mary (Mollie) Easley, daughter of a farmer in the community. There he built a small home and later added a gin and mill, then several houses, and finally a store. The village was named Byrd Town. Later he moved his family to Detroit, Texas, where he engaged in the mercantile business for a time, and then in 1901 moved to Oklahoma Territory, where he lived until 1913, finally going to Midlothian, Texas. He and his wife celebrated their golden wedding anniversary there in 1929.

---

*Compiled by Orlean Ehrlich 12-1-71, revised by Louise Garland 9-19-75.

Edward Byrd died at the age of eighty-eight in 1943. Mollie Easley Byrd died in 1947 at the age of eighty-seven.

David Harold Byrd was born in Detroit, Texas, on April 24, 1900, the youngest of a family of five boys and three girls (four of the sons and one of the daughters being deceased). On June 8, 1935, he married Mattie (Martha) Caruth of Dallas, a member of another illustrious pioneer family. They have two sons, David Harold Byrd, Jr., born in 1937, and Caruth Clark Byrd, born in 1941; one grandson, David Harold Byrd III, born in 1963, son of Harold, Jr., and Roberta Byrd, and one granddaughter, Martha Sue, born in 1965, daughter of Caruth and Wilda Byrd. Mattie Caruth Byrd died in 1972.

II. Beginnings In Oil

After attending school at Trinity University, where he served with the S.A.T.C. in 1917-19 during World War I, and two years at the University of Texas, where he majored in geology, Harold Byrd began work in the oil fields, locating first at Burkburnett, Texas, at the height of its boom. Later he accepted a position at Mexia with Colonel A.E. Humphreys, known as "king of the wildcatters." While with the Humphreys' interest, he learned all phases of the industry, with special emphasis on drilling activities. He left the Mexia Field in 1924 for San Antonio, where he became manager and geologist for the Old Dominion Oil Company. In 1925, he moved to Brownwood and established himself as a consulting geologist and drilling contractor, operating there until 1929. It was during this period that Byrd instituted and completed an extensive campaign of drilling wildcat wells throughout central West Texas, his earnestness of purpose and daring helping him through fifty-six dry holes before attaining success with his first producer along the Balcones Fault zone. It was from this experience that he earned the name of "Dry Hole Byrd." The turning point of his career came in 1928 with his discovery of the Santa Anna Field in Coleman County, Texas. In successive years he and his associates brought in the West Ira Field in Scurry County, the Byler Pool and the Baker Gas Field in Brown County, and the Shipley Pool in Ward County.

Harold Byrd was one of the oil pioneers of the East Texas Field, at one time having owned 50,000 acres of leases in the Lathrop, Kilgore, Bateman, Overton and Henderson areas, stretching from Gladewater to Henderson. The operations of Harold Byrd and Jack Frost in that locality, resulting in production of approximately 4,000 barrels of oil daily from some 492 wells, constituted the basis of the organization of Byrd-Frost, Inc., which was established in 1931 with Byrd as its president. That company operated extensively in East Texas and later the Four Corners area located in Colorado, New Mexico, Arizona, and Utah, and was credited with discovery in the latter area of the Kutz Canyon, Boundary Butte, Dove Creek, Largo, McElmo, and Clear Creek Fields. In the Clear Creek Field Byrd-Frost, Inc. drilled the "highest above sea level" well in the world; and Byrd was one of the founders of the Utah Natural Gas Company which built a pipeline to Salt Lake City, 118 miles away, to handle its production.

In 1947, Harold Byrd founded two personal companies, Byrd Oil Corporation and B-H Drilling Corporation. Later he organized the Byrd Uranium Corporation for the exploration of uranium and vanadium. In 1956, he sold his controlling interest in all three, and resigned as president and director. Byrd Oil Corporation later became Bayview and Mobil Oil Corporation bought its assets. Other companies which he helped establish and of which he was an officer and director were Plains Production Company—

president from 1931 to 1952; Talco Asphalt & Refining Company—partner from 1937 to 1938; Long Lake Production Company—president from 1938 to 1949; McConnell Drilling Corporation—president from 1947 to 1953; Colorado Carbonics, Inc.—president from 1948 to 1956; Inland Refining Company and Anco Gas Corporation—vice-president from 1952 to 1953. In 1950, he was one of the founders of Three States Natural Gas Company and served as a director until 1956. Byrd-Frost, Inc. and Plains Production Company were absorbed by Three States in 1952, and it in turn was purchased by Delhi-Taylor Oil Corporation in 1961. Tenneco and Continental bought out Delhi.

D.H. Byrd does not presently have a personally-owned company as the vehicle for his wide-spread oil and gas holdings, but he engages independently or jointly throughout the United States in such operations. He also has corporate connections in the United States, Mexico, Honduras, and Australia, presently with such organizations as Petrolera "MYM," S.A., Petroleos Hondurenos, S.A., and Delhi-Australian Petroleum, Ltd. Until 1963 he also operated a rotary drilling rig, principally for his own use.

During World War II Byrd was appointed to the Panel of Arbitrators, Inter-American Arbitration Commission, and to the Industry Advisory Committee for Petroleum and Petroleum Products, District 3. He was also a member of the East Texas Oil Association and president of the Independent Petroleum Association of Texas. He is currently a member of the following organizations connected with the oil and gas industry: Dallas Wildcat Committee, Dallas Geological and Geophysical Society, Texas Mid-Continent Oil and Gas Association (director), American Petroleum Institute, American Association of Petroleum Geologists, National Oil Scouts and Landmen's Association, and associate member of International Oil Scouts Association.

III. Connection With Aviation & Civil Air Patrol

In addition to his varied activities in the oil business, D.H. Byrd has labored unceasingly toward furthering a comprehensive study and constructive program for the aviation industry. He was interested in aviation from its early development and was one of the first men in Texas to own his own plane. He purchased the initial one, an Eaglerock made in Colorado Springs, in 1926; then a few years later bought a Stinson, which Colonel Art Goebel, the famous flyer who won the Honolulu race, taught him to fly. Over the years he has owned fifty-eight aircraft, both large and small, nine of which he donated to Civil Air Patrol during World War II and five of which were lost. For the past forty years he has owned a succession of Lockheed 12's and Lodestars, which he used for business and personal flights. In 1958, he donated a Twin Beech to the Texas Department of Public Safety for use by the Texas Rangers. As an appreciation of this gesture, and many others, they made him an honorary captain in their organization. On January 5, 1960, he was appointed a Special Texas Ranger, which commission was renewed for several bienniums. In 1964 Byrd donated a Lockheed Lodestar to the Department in the name of the Texas Rangers.

Byrd organized and operated three commercial aircraft services: one, the Byrd Air Transport Company, from 1944 to 1949; another, the Texas Air Transport, Inc., in 1946; and a third, the Executive Flyers, Inc., from 1955 to 1957.

He has also been responsible for many aviation concerns establishing plants in the environs of Dallas. He was one of the original founders and has been a continuous director of Temco Aircraft Corporation until 1970 when he was made director emeritus. That company expanded its facilities to comprise several plants at Dallas, Garland, and Greenville, Texas, and in 1960 merged with Ling-Altec to form Ling-Temco Electronics, Inc. In August, 1961, it in turn merged with Chance-Vought to form Ling-Temco-Vought, Inc., one of the present-day leaders in the electronics and aerospace fields. In July, 1957, Byrd organized and became chairman of the board of Space Corporation, which now has four subsidiaries, and specializes in propulsion and ground control test equipment for jet engines, aerospace ground support equipment, and custom-made, heavy-duty trucks, and was made chairman of its board. Both of these companies have important government contracts.

Concurrently with his civic and industrial endeavors, Byrd served as a member of the Texas Civil Aeronautics Commission (under Governors Allred and O'Daniel), making a complete survey of the state airport system and attending regional and other aviation conferences at all levels. In this connection he was also appointed a member of the Texas World's Fair Commission from 1937-1939.

Byrd was instrumental in obtaining for Dallas the Lockheed Modification Center, and in 1940 made a successful bid for the location of Hensley Field, U.S. Naval Air Base, at nearby Grand Prairie—both projects contributing largely to the success of the United States and its allies in World War II. On October 16, 1966, the occasion of Hensley Field's 25th anniversary, he received the Distinguished Service Award from the Naval Air Station for his part in founding this pilot training center.

Although no individual person or factor may be given full credit for the eminent position of Dallas in the aviation limelight, D.H. Byrd has contributed significantly to making Dallas the "Aviation Crossroads" of the North

American continent. It was under his leadership, as chairman of the City Aviation Board from 1937 to 1940, that the enlarged facilities at Love Field were put through to a successful completion. Byrd not only spent freely from his personal funds to publicize the necessity for these airport installations and later improvements, but he has been a powerful force in seeing that Love Field maintains the highest national rating possible as a Class "A" airport. On October 25, 1957, on the occasion of the extension of Love Field and the opening of its new terminal building, D.H. Byrd was honored by the Pioneers Club with the presentation of a plaque reading:

> Tribute to D. Harold Byrd, pioneer business airman, sponsor of Love Field and Hensley Field in the hard years, patron and benefactor of civil and military aviation, whose generous and dynamic support has contributed much to the art and science of aeronautics in his community, his State and the Nation.

Byrd has continued to serve the aviation needs of Dallas as a member of The Aviation Committees of the Dallas Chamber of Commerce and the Greater Dallas Planning Council and on the Dallas City-Council Civil Defense and Disaster Commission. On April 16, 1962, he was elected a charter member of the Dallas Aviation Council, affiliate of the Aviation Committee of the Chamber of Commerce, having for its purpose the protection and promotion of Love Field. He is also a member of the National Aeronautic Association, the National Intercollegiate Flying Association, the University Aviation Association, and an associate member of the Air Force Association. For several years he was a Liaison Officer of the Air Force Academy. In recognition of his services in that capacity, he was awarded on August 10, 1959 a certificate of honorary membership in The Falcon Foundation.

Another tribute to Byrd's part in the field of aviation was a plaque given to him by Pan American on March 17, 1961, which reads as follows:

> Having made valuable and significant contributions to World Air Transport and to the furtherance of international understanding, D. Harold Byrd is hereby appointed to membership in The Clipper Club.

On December 30, 1963, Byrd was elected to the Board of Advisors of the newly-established "Air Museum" in California. The plaque proclaiming this membership had this inscription in green, "In Honor of Rare Birds." This was in appreciation of his financial assistance in obtaining for the museum a Spitfire from the World War II battlefields of Southeast Asia, and which had been donated by the King of Thailand. On June 18, 1965, Byrd received a similar honor from the chancellor of the University of Texas, who appointed him honorary chairman of the newly-created advisory board of their history of aviation project.

Through the association with his cousin, the late Admiral Richard E. Byrd, Harold Byrd became interested in the former's many polar expeditions and contributed in many ways to those projects. Two of his most cherished possessions are a flag flown over the South and North Poles and a geological specimen taken from the Harold Byrd Mountains, a range discovered by Admiral Byrd 160 miles south of the South Pole and named in honor of his cousin in appreciation for his support. In 1936, during the Texas Centennial, Harold Byrd sponsored the "Little America Exhibit," complete with Curtis-Condor plane and a sample of all supplies and accoutrements used in making up the Admiral's expedition into Little America. Five of the personnel in charge of the exhibit had been members of the group that went into the Polar Regions. They all held Congressional Medals. During the first year of the current polar exploration, conducted under the name, "Operation Deep Freeze," Harold Byrd contributed a substantial part of the expenses of two CAP cadets who were participating in the project. He also contributes regularly to the Antarctic Exploration Society, Inc.

On July 9, 1962, the Department of the Navy awarded D. Harold Byrd a citation, expressing their appreciation and tribute for his connection with the Naval Air Station at Hensley Field and his contribution to the Polar expeditions of Admiral Richard E. Byrd. The plaque reads as follows:

> Long-time friend of the Navy—and particularly of Naval aviation—Colonel D. Harold Byrd was the moving force behind the pre-World War II effort which culminated in the establishment of Hensley Field as a Naval Air Station in the Dallas area. The bonds of friendship with the Navy go back to Colonel Byrd's association with and support of Rear Admiral Richard E. Byrd in the latter's Navy polar expeditions. In thus supporting his cousin's expeditions, Colonel Byrd was a contributor to later projects under Navy sponsorship in connection with Operation Deep Freeze. The Navy is proud to pay tribute to this patriotic American whose time and talents have always been willingly offered in support of the National Defense, often at great personal sacrifice.
>
> (Signed) - Fred Korth, Secretary of the Navy.

As a further honor, the Departments of the Navy and Defense invited Colonel Byrd to be a member of an official party that visited the Antarctic continent in February of 1963, as a commemorative tribute to Admiral Byrd. Using McMurdo Sound as the base of operations, flights were made to the South Pole, Byrd Station, Scott Station, and the Harold Byrd Mountains, where first photographs were taken of this range. More than 35,000 miles were traversed, mostly by jet aircraft, in the twelve-day journey, the fastest trip to that date made to the South

Pole and back. He received two certificates as a member of South Pole societies.

Following his return from the Antarctic, Colonel Byrd was nominated by Commander Richard E. Byrd, Jr., to serve as a director in the Antarctic Associates, Inc., an organization started during Admiral Byrd's lifetime but recently reactivated, whose purpose is designed to help carry on his work and make his material and records available for scientific and educational use in the public interest.

Perhaps the one organization with which Harold Byrd has been most widely identified and acclaimed is the Civil Air Patrol, which he and a small group of other alert citizens established in Washington on December 1, 1941, just six days before Pearl Harbor. Director of Defense Fiorello La Guardia, under President Roosevelt, appointed Byrd as Commander of the Texas Wing. For the duration of the war, Byrd guided the various activities conducted by Civil Air Patrol in his state, including border patrol, tow-target and antiaircraft training, radar testing, forest fire patrol, courier service, search and rescue missions, anti-sabotage patrol of power lines, etc., and the enlistment of preflight training for thousands of Army Air Force aviation cadets. As another important wartime service, CAP also established and operated antisubmarine patrol bases, and Byrd assumed personal command of the base at Beaumont, Texas. He was commissioned a Colonel in 1943, at the time CAP was transferred from the Office of Civilian Defense to the Department of War and placed under the supervision of the Army Air Force.

Following his tour of duty as Texas Wing Commander from 1941 to 1948, Colonel Byrd served as Southwestern Regional Commander from 1948 to 1953. Also in 1948 he was named vice-chairman of the national executive board, with General Carl Spaatz, USAFR, as chairman. Both served in these positions until April, 1959, when Spaatz retired and Byrd was elected chairman. Byrd retired as chairman in April, 1960, at which time he was made an honorary chairman of the board and a lifetime member in the Civil Air Patrol. In June, 1965, Byrd, along with other past board chairmen, was made a "chairman emeritus," with authority to attend all meetings of the national board and the national executive committee. He is also a member of the national advisory board and the national nominating committee. On July 11, 1970, he was promoted to the rank of brigadier general, CAP, chairman emeritus, by the national board.

Colonel Byrd was one of the incorporators of Civil Air Patrol, Inc., and helped obtain the passage of Public Law 476 at the 79th Congress on July 1, 1946, by which it obtained its national charter. He also assisted in having the CAP designated an auxiliary of the Air Force, through the passage of Public Law 557 by the 80th Congress on May 26, 1948. As chairman of the National Legislative Committee of CAP, Colonel Byrd took an active part in furthering other legislation for the benefit of the organization, two of which were the Supply Bill, passed in 1954, and the Compensation Bill, passed in 1956. He has lead several attempts to obtain financial aid from the Texas Legislature, and finally, in 1971, was successful and secured passage of a bill establishing the Texas Civil Air Patrol Commission. At its first meeting, he was elected its chairman.

Following World War II, Colonel Byrd with Colonel Earle L. Johnson lead in the establishment of the Cadet Program in CAP. Later in 1948, following the precept of Canada, Colonel Byrd helped initiate the International Air Cadet Exchange, whereby outstanding CAP cadets from the United States exchange visits with aviation students of other nations. This program is designed to encourage and promote good will among the youth of the participating countries through the mutual interest of aviation. Byrd has made several trips to Europe and South America to aid in this program and has personally assisted and participated in many of the tour arrangements, both in Texas and at national level. His last such trip was to London in April, 1958. He has worked very closely with the Air Cadet League of Canada, in which he holds an honorary life membership, and often attended its annual meetings as one of CAP's representatives.

Colonel Byrd's monetary contributions to CAP included such activities as Wing and Regional Communication supplies and special events, Texas Drill Team, and the Deep Freeze project to the South Pole. He has also been interested in the aviation education program, purchasing many sets of manuals and film strips and distributing them to Texas schools and CAP units for their use. For many years he has assisted, both personally and financially, in the entertainment of the foreign cadets visiting Texas and contributed many scholarships to deserving American cadets. In 1969 he furnished a lounge area for the National Headquarters Building at Maxwell Air Force Base, which has been designated the D.H. Byrd Room.

Among his many honors of recognition for his Civil Air Patrol service are: citation from the War Department for service in CAP during 1941-45; appointment in 1947 as a member of the Army Advisory Board, Fourth Army Headquarters; resolution passed by the Texas Legislature, commending the Texas Wing of CAP under Colonel Byrd's direction for its part in the defense of the state during World War II; Antisubmarine Coastal Patrol, Missing Aircraft Search, and Courier Ribbons; Relock Service Ribbon; plaque in appreciation of meritorious service from Wing Commanders, Southwest Region, 4/27/52; the Distinguished Service Award Certificate and appointment as life member, CAP, May 5, 1954; International Exchange Ribbon on June 4, 1959; Distinguished Service Ribbon with Bronze Clasp on November 1, 1959; and life membership in the Patrol Club, National Headquarters, CAP, on the same date. Also, in 1957, the CAP established three aeronautical engineering scholarships of $4,000 each, to be awarded to deserving CAP cadets in the names of General Spaatz, General Beau, and Colonel Byrd.

There have been other additional honors accorded Colonel Byrd by the Civil Air Patrol organization itself: The Texas Wing in October, 1961, established a special cadet unit, comprised of outstanding cadets who have graduated from cadet status but not yet ready for senior membership, which was called "The D. Harold Byrd Squadron." A plaque was presented him on January 25, 1962 by National Headquarters, honoring him for distinguished service as Commander of the Texas Wing from December, 1941 to May, 1948. In 1965, life membership was standardized by the national board, and Colonel Byrd received a plaque recognizing his distinguished service while chairman of the said board.

In April, 1966, at the Southwest Regional Conference, he was honored with a salute as one of CAP's founders and best friends, and was given a plaque "For his long devotion and interest in Civil Air Patrol and his close association with the Southwest Region."

On May 24, 1963, during the Aviation Writers & Publishers Convention in Dallas, the U.S. Air Force presented to Colonel Byrd its Scroll of Appreciation, reading as follows:

> For rendering meritorious service to the United States Air Force from Dec. 1941 to April, 1960. Motivated by a strong sense of patriotism, Mr. Byrd played a major part in the successful operation of the Texas Wing, Civil Air Patrol, throughout World War II. After the war he assisted in the incorporation of the Civil Air Patrol and its designation as an Auxiliary of the Air Force. Mr. Byrd helped initiate the International Air Cadet Exchange and worked closely with the Air Cadet League of Canada. The many scholarships established or supported by Mr. Byrd have aided countless cadets in the

attainment of additional training and higher education. His contributions of material and personal aircraft to the use of Civil Air Patrol materially aided in the performance of its mission. The distinctive accomplishments of Mr. Byrd have earned for him the sincere gratitude of the United States Air Force.

(Signed) - Curtis E. Lemay
Chief of Staff

(Signed) - Eugene M. Zuckert
Secretary of the Air Force

Another tribute was on June 3, 1972, when the National Executive Committee of the Civil Air Patrol voted unanimously to accept the nominating board's ten nominations to the CAP "Hall of Honor," one of which was Brigadier General D. Harold Byrd, and on the evening of September 29, 1972, at the National Convention in Dallas, Texas at the Statler-Hilton Hotel, Brigadier General Byrd and nine others were inducted into the CAP "Hall of Honor" in recognition of outstanding service to the Civil Air Patrol. Pictures and bronze plaques were hung in the Hall of Honor at the Air Force Museum, Wright-Patterson Air Force Base, Ohio.

IV. Philanthropies and Scholarships

In addition to his activities in the oil business, aviation, investments, farming and ranching, finance, and other diversified enterprises, D.H. Byrd finds time to devote to organizations which are dedicated to the general welfare and human service. His philanthropies are many and varied. He has a deep sense of responsibility to the community in which he lives and lends his support to many civic, state, and national charities. Among his special institutions are the Texas Scottish Rite Hospital for Crippled Children, the American Red Cross, the Dallas United Fund, and the Miracle at Pentecost Foundation, a project of Mrs. Byrd. He also considers and lends support to innumerable worthwhile inventions and projects which will aid human development or scientific progress. In 1953, the Byrd Foundation was formed exclusively for charitable, scientific, religious, literary or educational purposes, and both the Foundation and Byrd personally have contributed generously to many worthy causes too numerous to itemize.

A significant aspect of Harold Byrd's contributions has been the number of scholarships he has established. Many young students or former students of various universities or colleges can attribute their chance for a higher education to the monetary aid and spiritual encouragement of Byrd.

He is honorary president and patron of the University of Texas Longhorn Band, and each year three outstanding band members receive the "Harold Byrd Awards" for leadership. Through the Byrd Foundation, he makes an annual contribution for scholarships of band applicants. In addition to these, he has provided many other boys and girls with the means to attend the University of Texas, Southern Methodist University, Trinity University, Kemper Military Academy, Greenhill School (a private secondary school), and others.

Byrd's support of all phases of the University of Texas system is well known by its alumni and throughout Texas. Among his recent contributions was a $10,000 donation to "kick off" the drive for the assembly room designated as the "T" Lettermen's Lounge. On January 13, 1960, in recognition for this and his other gifts to the university, he was named an honorary "Letterman." On November 24, 1961, he was appointed a member of the Special Gifts Committee. He is a director of the Longhorn Club and the

Cotton Bowl Association; a member of the Advisory Committee of the Forty Acres Club; and a lifetime, honorary vice-president of the University of Texas Dads' Association, as well as a life member of the Ex-Students Association. He is also a member of the Board of Trustees of Schreiner Institute, Kerrville, Texas, and at one time was a vice-president of the Fathers' Association at Culver Military Academy. In December, 1965, in recognition for his past gifts to The University of Texas, he was elected to the Chancellor's Council as a "Founding" member. On October 14, 1966, the Ex-Students Association presented to Harold Byrd the Distinguished Alumnus Award, honoring ex-students of The University of Texas who through distinguished service in their chosen profession have brought honor to their alma mater, and through personal dedication have fostered the ideals of The Ex-Students' Association.

During his active participation in the Civil Air Patrol, Colonel Byrd sponsored several scholarship programs for the cadets and senior members. In 1956, he agreed to contribute an annual award for a flight scholarship to a cadet from the Dallas Squadron; and during that first year, when two applicants could not be decided between, awarded them each a scholarship! In the same year, believing strongly in the efficacy of the chaplain's program in CAP, the Byrd Foundation contributed over $3,000 to one of the regional chaplains (Rudolph Renfer) to further his studies in Europe. In 1947, Colonel Byrd established the "D. Harold Byrd Leadership Awards," by which each year three outstanding persons in CAP were selected to receive $500 each—one from the wing commanders; one from the senior personnel; and one from the cadets. Also, in 1957, he gave a scholarship to Culver Military Academy, the selectee being from the CAP Cadet ranks there and the recipient receiving $1500 a year for three years. This student on graduation in June, 1960, obtained appointment as an honor student to the USAF Academy.

D.H. Byrd is also very active in church affairs, being a deacon in the First Presbyterian Church of Dallas. He, Mrs. Byrd, and their two sons have made many generous contributions to the furtherance of its program and growth, one notable example being the donation of an entire room, complete with kitchen and full-size stage and with a capacity of 400 persons, designated as the "Byrd Fellowship Hall."

V. Other Activities

Harold Byrd does not confine himself to any one line of business or endeavor, but engages in many diversified projects, in which he has either a management position or a heavy financial interest. They comprise farms, ranches and feedlots, oil and gas operations, trusts and foundations, financial and investment companies, industrial and residential real estate, recreational projects, and miscellaneous industrial, manufacturing and commercial corporations. He maintains an office at 1110 Tower Petroleum Building, Dallas, which is the hub of his activities and from which he guides the affairs and destinies of his many enterprises.

In spite of his busy business and civic life, Harold Byrd finds time for many sporting and social activities. He, and often his entire family, and their friends engage in hunting and fishing expeditions to all parts of the United States, Canada, and Mexico, traveling often by private plane. In November and December of 1963, and again in August and September, 1965, he extended these boundaries by safaris to Central and East Africa; and in April, 1964, he and his son, Caruth, added to their laurels the acquisition of two polar bears in Alaska and, in 1969, he and General Jimmy Doolittle hunted in the wilds of Sumatra. In May, 1973, he and his son, Caruth, spent two weeks on safari in the Republic of Botswana, South Africa, where they added a total of fifteen animals to his collection for his "Trophy Room," some of which are springbok, wildebeest, gemsbok, heartsbeast, ostrich, impala, tcessabee, lechwe, kudu and cape buffalo.

As indication of national interest in his activities and in recognition of his wide-spread and varied accomplishments, Harold Byrd has been honored by the T.V. industry in the presentation of four televised programs. The first was an account of his life, prepared by Jackit Productions, Inc., as one of their "Sweet Success" series, during the period from December, 1959, through June, 1960, telecasts being made all during 1961. The second was the production in October, 1961, of "P.M. West," under the title, "Texas Facts and Fiction," in which he shared the spotlight with other Texas millionaires Jim Ling, Erik Jonsson, and Edward Marcus. The third was in May, 1968, when KRLD-TV sponsored a program called "Successful Texans," and the fourth was aired by the British Broadcasting System in London in 1968.

On February 21, 1962, Byrd was elected a member of the Corporate Board of the College of Osteopathic Medicine and Surgery, Des Moines, Iowa, and in June of that year, was awarded an honorary Doctor of Science from the same college. However, in September, 1966, he had to resign from the board due to the press of other demands.

On August 6, 1962, and again in 1964, Byrd was appointed a member of the Advisory Council for development of the Graduate Research Center of the Southwest in

Dallas, a scholastic facility created for graduate training of highly skilled technical students leading to doctorate degrees. In this connection he made a substantial pledge for the continuing financial support of the work in the Center.

On March 7, 1964, Byrd was appointed a member of the newly-established Potentate's Advisory Board of the Hella Temple, this group consisting of forty outstanding personalities of Dallas, and designed to be a "top-flight show case" for the Shrine. On October 20, 1969, he was elected to Bodies A. & ASR in Ceremonial of Investiture for honorable service.

He is listed in *Who's Who in America* and in *Dun & Bradstreet's* "Top Management." His diversified memberships, not mentioned elsewhere in this article, comprise the following business, civic, cultural, educational, fraternal, service and sports associations: Better Business Bureau, Dallas Citizens Council, Dallas Citizens Traffic Commission, Dallas Council on World Affairs, Dallas Crime Commission, Pan-American Reception Committee for State Fair of Texas, Citizens Hospital Advisory Committee, Dallas Historical Society, Dallas Zoological Association, Trinity Improvement Association (director), Newcomen Society in North America, Trinity Tiger 60 Club (charter member), Mustang Club, Inc., Kappa Kappa Psi (Bank fraternity, honorary member), Sigma Delta Psi (honorary athletic fraternity), Hella Temple, Scottish Rite Bodies, Elks, Bonehead Club of Dallas, Advisory Board of Soroptimist Crippled Children's Camp, Circle 10 of Boy Scouts of America (member-at-large), YMCA, National Football Foundation and Hall of Fame (life and charter member), Sportmen's Club of Texas, Inc., Wildlife Society, Presidents Health Club Spas, Inc. (charter member), Navy League of U.S. (life member),

Dallas Woods and Waters Club, the Explorers Club of N.Y., Smithsonian Society of Associates, and Texas State Society of Washington.

His social clubs include the following: Admirals Club, Brookhollow Golf, Calyx, Thalia, City, Club Imperial, Dallas Athletic and Country (life member), Dallas Club, Dallas Country Club, Executives' Dinner Club, Rafters, Knife and Fork Club, Petroleum Club, Skynight Club, Terpsichorean Club, Preston Trail Golf Club, The Lancers Club, (all of Dallas); Austin Club, Deck Club, and Headliners Club (Austin, Texas); Koon Kreek Klub (Athens, Texas); Petroleum Club (Houston, Texas); Tanglewood-on-the-Lake Country Club (Lake Texoma, life member); Balboa Bay Club (Newport Beach, Calif.); Garden of the Gods Club (Colorado Springs); USAF "100 Club" and Officers Club (AF Academy, honorary life member) and Wings Club (New York City) and Tres Vidas (founder-member) of Acapulco, Mexico.

Mattie Caruth Byrd died in February, 1972, and on February 14, 1974 General Byrd married Mavis Barnett Heath, widow of the former United States Ambassador to Sweden, William Womack Heath, who also served as Secretary of State and Chairman of the Board of Regents of The University of Texas. They have two daughters, Cynthia Heath Ray and Linda Heath Hester Nelson; three granddaughters, Mavis, Melodie, and Julia Ray; two grandsons, Bill and Dylan Hester.